lhy, God W|
Y WON'T YOU A
here so muc
WHY GOT
M, GOD? Why, God? why, God? Why, God?
God? IHY AM I SO ANXIO
Why, Go

WHY,

THE 4 MOST IMPORTANT TRUTHS

GOD?

GOD? why did my wife get cancer?
won't my pain end?
should I belie d? Why, God WHY, GOD
do bad thing ee to good people?
WHY
lhy, God WHY, GOD? ust God?
WHY
hy is my life falling apart? |
Y, God? HY, God!

Josh Combs

THE RIVER CHURCH
REACH | GATHER | GROW

For Adalyn and Maelyn.

For Dee.

For Ira.

For Jerry.

For Raymond and Sonny.

For Davey.

For Chelsea.

For Uncle Tom.

For Addison.

For Kip.

For Luke.

And for all of those who love and miss them dearly.

Jen and I love you.

WHY, God? WHY WAS I ABUSE

HY, GOD? Why God?

hy won't why don't you lov

Why do awful things happen?

WHY, GOD? why does the Bib

HY, GOD? WHY, GOD? WH

OD? Why is this happening to

Y GOD?

why should I trust you, God?

things happen to innocent

WHY, GOD?

don't you show yourself?

WHY, G

Y WON'T YOU ANSWER MY PRAYERS? WHY

WHY,

WHY, GOD? Why doesn't God save everyone

hy did you create me, God? GOD

is my life falling apa

Y DOES GOD LET BAD

Why, GOD Why should I

d you let this happen?

od? WHY AM I SO ANXIO

why do bad things happen to go

WHY, GOD?

is there so much darkness? wife get cancer?

CONTENTS

Why, God? WHY WAS I ABUSE
HY, GOD? Why, God?
hy won't why don't you lov
Why do awful things happen?
WHY, GOD? why does the Bib
HY, GOD? WHY, GOD? WH
OD? Why is this happening to
Y GOD?
HY GOD? why should I trust you, God?
things happen to innocent
WHY GOD?
don't you show yourself? WHY G
Y WON'T YOU ANSWER MY PRAYERS? WHY
WHY,
Why doesn't God save everyone
hy did you create me, God? GOD
is my life falling apa
TY DOES GOD LET BAD
Why, God? Why should I
d you let this happen?
od? WHY AM I SO ANXIOU
why do bad things happen to go
WHY, GOD?
is there so much darkness?
wife get cancer?

INTRODUCTION

"People are born for trouble as readily as sparks fly up from a fire."

Job 5:7 (NLT)

I've heard it said before that we are either in crisis, coming out of crisis, or headed into crisis. I suppose that can be a bit depressing, but wherever you are in relation to a crisis, this book is for you.

In almost 25 years of pastoral ministry, I've had hundreds of lunch meetings, but none as powerful as the one I shared with a friend in the spring of 2017. What I assumed would be a relatively normal lunch conversation, changed my life forever.

I was meeting with Russell, a brilliant man, whose intellect can be a bit intimidating. His brain power and sheer knowledge of life is amazing. I always tease him as being the smartest man to ever come out of Arkansas. He is also one of the most caring and genuine people I have ever met.

As we walked into the restaurant, I was excited about eating one of my favorite meals. Russell greeted me and asked, sincerely, how my day was. It was a Tuesday, and we were in the middle of merging three large churches into one. Tuesdays were my most challenging day of the week. The majority of the day was spent in meetings: elder meetings, all staff meetings, team meetings, event meetings... you get the idea. It was a mentally, emotionally, and spiritually demanding day. I don't recall on that particular Tuesday who or what was agitating me, but something was. When Russell asked how I was doing, I unloaded. Not recalling specifics, I imagine I vented about staff, communication, impending decisions, the upcoming Easter production, and I'm sure a slew of other issues. Russell kindly listened and responded caringly, but then it hit me like a Mack truck.

I vividly recall stopping dead in the tracks of my verbal tirade. My friend's only child, Adalyn, was in the hospital! Since her birth just a few months earlier, she had left the hospital for a very brief homecoming, only to return in worse condition. Russell's wife, Heather, was living at the hospital, advocating and caring for their daughter. Heather literally never left. As a couple, they were staying in the nearby Ronald McDonald House. Like an anvil falling from Heaven, God crushed me. Instantly, I realized how much of a self-absorbed jerk I was.

While I was whining about work, my dear friend's daughter was fighting for her life. In that moment, I was so sick to my stomach I didn't care to eat. I quickly tried to change the subject and asked Russell how he was doing. He began to cry. I knew he had some heavy things to talk to me about. We ordered, got our food, and found an empty booth in the midst of a very busy lunch hour. The noise of the bustling restaurant seemed to just fade away. As long as I live, I'll never forget the conversation we had over the next few minutes. Tears began to stream down Russell's face as he asked me, "Why?"

I braced to answer questions about his daughter and her medical struggles, but this sweet man wasn't asking about Adalyn. That very day, friends that he and Heather had met in the hospital had lost their child and another couple was nearing the end of the journey with theirs. Russell looked me straight in the eyes and asked, "Why are these sweet, innocent children dying? Why is God letting this happen?" He wasn't ranting or yelling; he was asking, pleading for the truth. We were sitting in an extremely busy place, surrounded by people, both sobbing. What could I tell him? What explanation could I give? What would comfort him or bring peace to his heart? And his question about God - how could

I defend or advocate for God? What rationale could I make that didn't sound too churchy or preachy? I felt hopelessly inadequate. Then, I felt deep in my soul the Holy Spirit simply say to me, "Tell him."

For the next few moments in my head, I argued with God. "Lord," I thought, "he might hate me. He might leave the church. Lord, the truth is really heavy and hard. The truth will hurt him. It will be too bitter of a pill to swallow. I'm sure you just want me to listen and care." I've never been a good listener, but I was fighting God for permission to just listen that day. Yet the Lord was adamant - tell Russell the truth.

"Russell," I said, "I need to go to the car to get my Bible. I'll be back in a second." I knew what the Lord wanted me to say, but I was afraid. I was scared of offending him, but deep down I was even more afraid of what he would think of me when I told him the truth. I didn't want to recklessly hurt my already hurting friend. I know the truth is not what most people want to hear or can handle hearing during their time of grief and crisis. This was different. Russell wanted answers and I had clearly sensed the still, small, mighty voice of God tell me to answer his question.

I walked to the car, grabbed my Bible, and then headed back into the restaurant. I sat down and flipped to a page with a sticky note I had scribbled some notes on. For the previous three or four years, I had written a series of notes in my Bible. Around 2013 or before, I can't really remember, the Lord had shown me in the Bible what I thought were the four most important truths in Scripture, in the world, and I would even say in the universe. At first, I thought this Biblical hypothesis may be just an extreme oversimplification. However, since writing them down, reading

Scripture, and checking them against God's final authority over and over again, I've become convinced that they are, in fact, the four most important truths.

That day, sitting in a booth surrounded by people taking a quick lunch break, we opened the Bible and began talking through these truths. My friend Russell listened. And being a preacher, I have a decent sense of when people are listening, when they are pretending to listen, and when they have checked out. He listened intently. He didn't protest. He didn't argue. We were handling heavy truths and he didn't buckle. I watched God illuminate profound realities for my friend and for me. I left that restaurant changed. I walked to my car and sobbed – a shaking, ugly cry that only God and I witnessed. God had used me that day to help my friend. God had also mercifully revealed my prideful, selfish heart.

This book is what I told him and what I believe the truth of the Scripture clearly and consistently teaches. Whatever trial or storm you are facing, or even victory you have gained, I believe that these four truths can transform you, sustain you, and carry you through to the finish line. They are the four most important truths and they are true for all time.

Truth #1 – God is in complete control.
Truth #2 – All things exist for God's glory.
Truth #3 – God's ways are not our ways.
Truth #4 – God loves you and me.

I want to end this introduction by adding a sincere and genuine warning label. When I was a child, one of my favorite books was *The Monster at the End of This Book: Starring Lovable, Furry Old Grover*. Grover was my favorite *Sesame Street* character. The premise of the book is that Grover is trying to stop the reader from turning the pages because there's a monster at the end of the book. In the end, the monster is just Grover. There isn't a monster at the end of *this* book, but there are some tough things right at the beginning.

Unlike Grover, who is trying in vain to keep the reader from turning the page, I am trying to encourage you and, in extreme cases, beg you to keep going. Proceed with caution, but please proceed. Keep reading and face, not a monster, but important truths. These truths aren't simple, easy, or without mystery, but they will be an anchor in the waves of grief, a firm foundation in an ever-changing world, the grid for a truly Biblical worldview, and peace when everything seems to go wrong.

Russell was ready for the truth, but you may not be. And that's okay. When you are, pick this book up and read it. Maybe *you* are ready, but your spouse or friend isn't. Timing is key. Even though this book is short, it might take you some time to read. Not because you're a slow reader, but because it might require time for you to process, and you might find some of these stories triggering. It's a little strange to say, but reading this book and believing the truths in it will take courage. "Courage is not the absence of fear, but rather the assessment that something else is more important than fear."[1] It is okay to be afraid, just know that *someone* (not something) else more important than fear awaits you. And that someone is God. King David wrote, "When I am afraid, I put my trust in you" (Psalm 56:3).

Prayer of confession and belief –

God, I want to encounter you for real. I want to see you and know you. As I draw near to you, I know that you draw near to me. Amen.

For further reading: Psalm 46

Why, God? WHY WAS I ABUSE

HY, GOD? Why, God?

hy won't why don't you lov

Why do awful things happen?

WHY, GOD? why does the Bib

HY, GOD? WHY, GOD? WH

OD? Why is this happening to r

Y GOD? W

why should I trust you, God?

HY, GOD? things happen to innocent ge

WHY, GOD?

don't you show yourself?

WHY G

Y WON'T YOU ANSWER MY PRAYERS? WHY

WHY,

VHY, GOD? Why doesn't God save everyone

hy did you create me, God? GOD

is my life falling apa

tY DOES GOD LET BAD

Why, God? Why should I I

d you let this happen?

od? WHY AM I SO ANXIOI

hy do bad things happen to go

WHY, GOD?

is there so much darkness? wife get cancer?

TRUTH #1
GOD IS IN COMPLETE CONTROL

"There is not a square inch in the whole domain of our human existence over which [God] who is Sovereign over all, does not cry, 'Mine!'"[2]

– Abraham Kuyper, theologian, journalist, and former prime minister of the Netherlands

"If there is a God, where was He? Why did He let that happen? Why didn't God stop it?" I was 20 years old, and it was just days after September 11, 2001, when a man angrily asked these questions. He wasn't talking to me, but I intended to regale him with a philosophical perspective that would illuminate his simple mind to the complex realities of the divine order. It didn't work. He didn't give a rip. He didn't care about the mysteries of free will and sovereignty. He just saw planes smash into the World Trade Center. He saw people engulfed in flames plunge to their death. He didn't want the musings of an amateur philosopher; he needed something more.

That may have been the first time I clearly heard the question, "Where was God?" but it wasn't the last. Since that day, I've heard the question repeated and rephrased: "If God is loving, why would He let that happen? Why didn't He show up? Couldn't He have stopped it?" Often in those moments of examination, many religious people try to defend God, as I did. They feel obligated to be God's defense attorney or publicist. The intention is to make God look good, be understandable, and sort of bring Him down to earth.

I've heard well-intentioned people say things like, "God didn't do that; that's the devil; God will never give you more than you can handle; God needed your child more than you; he is now a little angel; it isn't our place to ask why," or worse. In those moments of intense scrutiny, the faithful often fall back on empty expressions, platitudes, and clichés. It's fortune cookie philosophy or greeting card counseling with a religious twist. The thoughts may sound like they are in the Bible, but they lack substance and truth. Occasionally, people really want to know, "Where is God? Why didn't He stop this from happening?"

All of the doubts, frustration, confusion, and skepticism are circling around a couple of core questions: "Who is God? What is God like?" If God is… (fill in the blank however you want), but then something in life threatens that belief, we are faced with a problem. If my pastor, priest, teacher, parents, or grandma told me something about God when I was a kid that life now proves to be false or unreliable, what gives? Did they lie to me? Is everything I've learned about God wrong? Maybe what I've been taught about God is just a nice bedtime story or religious fairytale?

Our view of God often begins to be shaped in childhood. As life forces us to grow, change, and embrace more complex realities, sometimes our opinions about God from our youth just don't seem to keep up.[3] The God we learned about in Sunday School, catechism, or from grandma doesn't seem fit for the challenges and rigors of everyday life. We love grandma, but eventually we conclude that the god she told us about when we were a child is only for children. The Bible does talk about child-like faith, but that is different than a childish faith. Faith that doesn't mature and grow eventually sours.

For some, it is a first-semester science class in college that reveals their feeble faith. It very often prompts them to question God's existence (atheism). If not His existence, then His awareness or involvement in the world (agnosticism). The god of their childhood is incapable of standing up against the arguments of academia. For others, a personal crisis in life can bring doubts and disappointments to the surface. Even for so-called believers, the idea that God is good all the time seems questionable when life isn't so good. In our disappointment, we decide that who we've been believing in, singing about, and praying to isn't worthy of those things. Here's the point: what we believe about God shapes what we expect of Him.

If we believe God is just a character in some nice fairytale stories, of course He wouldn't belong in science, logic, and higher learning. If we believe God promises health and wealth to moral, well-behaved generous people, then we expect that from Him. Beliefs, views, and opinions about God are all over the map. And because of that, expectations of what God supposedly does and does not do vary wildly. Depending on your background, you could view God in a variety of different ways and base your expectations on that set of beliefs.

However, instead of having an accurate understanding of God, we often settle for a caricature of God. Like a caricature drawn at a county fair, we overemphasize and exaggerate one or two specific characteristics of God and ignore all others. Caricature artists will also create, imagine, or fabricate something that isn't even there. We can do the same with God. Here are a few caricatures that summarize what some people believe about God.

God: The Divine Santa Claus

Throughout the year, I do my best to stay off the naughty list and stay on his nice list. I do some charity work and try to be good, so that when I need to talk with him (pray), I can sit on his lap, give him my wish list, leave him out a plate of chocolate chip cookies, and BAM! Christmas day comes and Santa (god) delivers everything I told him I wanted and needed. It's all good until Santa doesn't give me what I want.

God: The First Responder

Crisis comes and we call 9-1-1. We pray, hoping god will answer the "phone." "God, if you get me out of this mess, I'll never do this again." Or "God, if you make this go away, I'll do [fill in the blank] for you." Often when the emergency is over, we forget our promise.

God: The Punisher

Angry and vengeful, god is waiting for you to make one wrong move and then he'll strike you dead. No mercy is his motto. People who view god like this often walk on religious eggshells completely terrified of god. This god has zero love, grace, mercy, or compassion. The punisher god is all law, order, and judgment. Don't you dare enter a church - the roof will certainly come crashing down on you!

God: Just Out Of Reach

In the 16th century, Michelangelo created one of the most renowned pieces of art in history. Lining the walls and across the ceiling of the Sistine Chapel are incredible frescos illustrating various events in the Bible. God is painted with a stern face, long gray hair and beard, and what looks to me like a pink robe. Even though you may not be a fan of fine art, this might be how you view god – as a distant, just out of reach being, floating around in the clouds.

God: The Old War Veteran

Each year in towns across America, military veterans march down mainstreet in their local parades. People stand and applaud. Communities remember the sacrifice of these brave men and women. Many times the veterans are old and frail and it may be hard to imagine them young and full of life. God the old war veteran is somebody who did some great and awesome things "back in the day." Where and what exactly he did we don't know, but there are some monuments and statues somewhere. He was useful and important, but those days have passed. As a courtesy, we'll stand and applaud for him on a holiday, usually Christmas and Easter.

God: The (hopefully) Heavyweight Champion of the World

God is locked in a cosmic battle with the devil and the forces of evil. These two are viewed as opposites and equals. In the end, we hope that god will win this divine tug of war.

God: Father to Unruly Children

God is shocked by the actions of Adam, Eve, and all of humanity. This idea of god sees him as scrambling to adapt. He is constantly operating in a Plan B-type mode. If people would just do right and "let go and let god" then everything would go to plan. God is a parent standing by totally helpless while his children run wild!

God: The Grandparent

God is like a fun grandparent. No rules, no bedtime, cookies, tons of fun, and endless snuggles. When something bad happens or rules are enforced or consequences for bad behavior are given, that just couldn't be god, because he is just love!

God: One Of Many

In Greek mythology, the gods lived on Mount Olympus. The god Cronos/Saturn eats all his kids, but Zeus/Jupiter escapes. He later returns and overthrows his father. Eventually, we get the demi-gods. The gods of Mt. Olympus were preceded by the Titans. Where did they come from? Perhaps they came from an endless line of humans who became gods, the God of the Bible or Jesus or whoever is just part of this big, violently unhappy family on Mt. Olympus.

God: The Absent-Minded Owner

God created something beautiful, and then rested. Is he sleeping? He must have washed his hands of it. Is god aware that things are literally spinning out of control? He's the driver completely asleep at the wheel of the universe. It must be up to us. Good luck folks. "May the odds be ever in your favor."[4]

Some of these descriptions are ridiculous and extreme, but I've met people who have explained God, maybe not in these exact terms, but in every one of those ways. Again, what we believe about God determines what we expect of Him.[5]

But what if we are wrong about God?

One of the best people in all of the Bible totally underestimated the Lord. His name was Job. His story is one of the most heartbreaking, troubling, and confusing of all time – at least to me. The book begins by describing Job as "blameless and upright, one who feared God and turned away from evil" (Job 1:1). The Bible continues, explaining that Job was an incredibly wealthy man and a loving father to ten children (seven sons and three daughters). But then the setting of the story unexpectedly shifts from earth to heaven.

God and Satan are having a conversation. As if that's not hard enough to wrap our minds around, God then draws Satan's attention to Job, whom He calls, "my servant." Satan challenges God, explaining that the only reason Job serves and loves Him is because God protects and blesses him. In response, God tells Satan that he can do what he wants to everything that belongs to Job, but he can't lay a finger on Job. God told Satan what he could and could *not* do. "Even the devil is God's devil,"[6] Martin Luther said. Satan had to come to God's throne for permission.

As the scene shifts back to earth, what would certainly be the worst day of Job's life begins to unfold. Before the sun sets, much of Job's wealth would be gone and all ten of Job's kids would be dead. Here is his response:

> Then Job arose and tore his robe and shaved his head and fell on the ground and worshiped. And he said, "Naked I 'came from mother's womb, and naked shall I return. The Lord gave, and the Lord has taken away; blessed be the name of the Lord." In all this Job did not sin or charge God with wrong. Job 1:20-22

WHAT? Wow. Job is an upright guy and these crises that came in rapid succession proved his character. But Job's story doesn't stop there. In the second chapter of the book there is another conversation between God and Satan. Again, God brings up Job, calling him "my servant." Satan argues with God that if he could touch Job's body, Job would abandon his integrity and curse

God. In response, God gives Satan authority over Job's body, but with the limit that Satan cannot kill Job. Keep in mind, Job is not privy to any of God and Satan's conversations.

Satan quickly and ruthlessly strikes Job with "loathsome sores from the sole of his foot to the crown of his head" (Job 2:7). Job becomes such a pitiable sight that his wife mercifully encourages him to "curse God and die." But Job refused. He responds, "'Shall we receive good from God, and shall we not receive evil?' In all of this Job did not sin with his lips" (Job 2:9-10). Job was sick, broke, and childless. Then his "friends" show up.

The next 35 chapters are a back-and-forth conversation between Job and his "friends." Notice I keep putting friends in quotation marks. Just imagine Job in this terrible state and these guys want to show up and give him some advice. More than that, they want to figure out what secret sin Job has been hiding that led to this calamity. Honestly, when you keep Job's emotional and physical condition in your mind, these "friends" are pretty cruel.

However, these conversations are brought to an abrupt end when God finally speaks to Job. And frankly, God isn't what Job expected. When God finishes, Job responds:

I had heard of you by the hearing of the ear, but now my eye sees you; therefore, I despise myself, and repent in dust and ashes. Job 42:5-6

What is interesting to me is that prior to God speaking, Job's one actually wise friend says, "God is great, and we know him not; the number of his years is unsearchable" (Job 36:26). God wasn't what Job or his friends had pictured in their minds.

When you hear a voice on the phone or on the radio or a podcast, unless you know the person or have seen a picture of them, naturally we create an image of what that person looks like. Rarely have any of the images I created in my head been accurate. Usually, they aren't even close! Job had heard things about God, but it turned out God was much bigger, grander, more powerful, and way beyond Job's simplistic ideas and imagination.

The same is true for us. We may "hear" things about God, and then create in our imagination what God must be like. And again, like the voice on the radio, we are way off! We rely on clichés, pithy sayings, and second-hand knowledge about God that falls abysmally short of reality. Very often our deeply held convictions about God are just plain wrong. The god we create in our heart, mind, and imagination isn't worthy of faith or reliance because he isn't real. It isn't the God of the Bible. We settle for worshiping or praying to a caricature of our own making. Like Job, we need a real encounter with God. We need to stop talking and let God speak.

What does God say about God?

Throughout human history, God has revealed Himself to all people in a few specific ways. Whether or not someone reads a Bible or encounters a missionary, basic knowledge about the character of God is accessible to all people for all time, across all languages, races, cultures, countries, and continents. Regardless of how remote a certain tribe may be, God has revealed Himself to them. These general revelations include creation, conscience, and eternity.

- Creation is a display of God's character. Romans says, "For what can be known about God is plain to them, because God has shown it to them. For his invisible attributes, namely, his eternal power and divine nature, have been clearly perceived, ever since the creation of the world, in the things that have been made. So they are without excuse." Romans 1:19-20

- As Creator and Designer, the Law of God has been hardwired into every person. Romans 2:15 says, "The law is written on their hearts." This is an inherent, basic sense of right and wrong that every person is born with. We call this conscience.

- Mankind's pursuit of immortality is a result of God implanting the very concept of eternity in our hearts. Ecclesiastes 3:11 says, God "has put eternity into man's heart." John Calvin wrote, "There is within the human mind, and indeed by natural instinct, an awareness of divinity."[7]

To reject the testimony of creation, moral absolutes, and the "awareness of divinity" is to reject God as He has graciously revealed Himself. The Apostle Paul, while explaining the one true God to the polytheists in Athens, explained that "they should seek God, and perhaps feel their way toward him and find him. Yet he is actually not far from each one of us" (Acts 17:27). God is not playing the unwinnable game of hide and seek.

God has allowed us to seek and find Him through the true stories and teachings of the Bible. "No prophecy," the Apostle Peter writes, "was ever produced by the will of man, but men spoke from God as they were carried along by the Holy Spirit" (2 Peter 1:21). God spoke to and through the writers of the Scripture. What they wrote was inspired (God-breathed). Often the Bible is called "God's Word," because it is God's *words* about Himself.

God's Word declares God to be in complete and sovereign control of the universe. Defining sovereignty, A.W. Pink writes, "We mean the supremacy of God, the kingship of God, the Godhood of God. To say that God is sovereign is to declare that God is God. To say that God is sovereign is to declare that He is the Most High, doing according to His will in the army of heaven, and among the inhabitants of the earth."[8]

Sovereignty means that God is the boss, the owner, and the ruler. Absolutely nothing in the universe happens that does not first come to His throne. Here are some verses from the Bible that affirm God's sovereign control of every inch of the universe.

> Yours, O Lord, is the greatness and the power and the glory and the victory and the majesty, for all that is in the heavens and in the earth is yours. Yours is the kingdom, O Lord, and you are exalted as head above all.
> 1 Chronicles 29:11

> He is unchangeable, and who can turn him back? What he desires, that he does. Job 23:13

> I know that you can do all things and that no purpose of yours can be thwarted. Job 42:2

The earth is the Lord's and the fullness thereof, the world and those who dwell therein. Psalm 24:1

The counsel of the Lord stands forever, the plans of his heart to all generations. Psalm 33:11

The Lord reigns. Psalm 97:1

Our God is in the heavens; he does all that he pleases. Psalm 115:3

Whatever the Lord pleases, he does, in heaven and on earth, in the seas and all deeps. Psalm 135:6

Many are the plans in the mind of a man, but it is the purpose of the Lord that will stand. Proverbs 19:21

His dominion is an everlasting dominion, and his kingdom endures from generation to generation; all the inhabitants of the earth are accounted as nothing, and he does according to his will among the host of heaven and among the inhabitants of the earth; and none can stay his hand or say to him, "What have you done?" Daniel 4:34-35

In him we have obtained an inheritance, having been predestined according to the purpose of him who works all things according to the counsel of his will. Ephesians 1:11

Hallelujah! For the Lord our God the Almighty reigns. Revelation 19:6

The Bible unapologetically claims God is in absolute control in Heaven and on earth. He has been ruling and reigning over the entire universe from the very beginning to the very end. And by saying the beginning and end, the Bible includes everything in between.

The Beginning...

When there was nothing, there was God. Then He spoke, and all that is came into being. That is the creation account of Genesis chapter 1. God is the creator, not a jump starter, facilitator, or participator. He is the origin of everything! There are no accidents or mistakes in creation. There is a divine designer.

The heavens are yours; the earth also is yours, the world and all that is in it, you have founded them. Psalm 89:11

I am the Lord, and there is no other; besides me there is no God...I form light and create darkness; I make well-being and create calamity; I am the Lord, who does all these things. Isaiah 45:5,7

Worthy are you, our Lord and God, to receive glory and honor and power, for you created all things, and by your will they existed and were created. Revelation 4:11

Rise and fall of Nations

Every nation and border has been set in place by the hand of the Almighty. The rise and fall of every nation and kingdom is by divine design.

He makes nations great, and he destroys them; he enlarges nations, and leads them away. Job 12:23

And he made from one man every nation of mankind to live on all the face of the earth, having determined allotted periods and the boundaries of their dwelling place. Acts 17:26

Weather

All weather, including "snow…rain…heat…[and] gloom of night"[9] are determined by the divine decree of God.

For to the snow he says, "Fall on the earth" likewise to the downpour, his mighty downpour….By the breath of God ice is given, and the broad waters are frozen fast. He loads the thick cloud with moisture; the clouds scatter his lightning. They turn around and around by his guidance, to accomplish all that he commands them on the face of the habitable world. Whether for correction or for his land or for love, he causes it to happen. Job 37:6, 10-13

You rule the raging of the sea; when its waves rise, you still them. Psalm 89:9

He it is who makes the clouds rise at the end of the earth, who makes lightnings for the rain and brings forth the wind from his storehouses. Psalm 135:7

He sends out his command to the earth; his words run swiftly. He gives snow like wool; he scatters frost like ashes. He hurls down his crystals of ice like crumbs; who can stand before his cold? He sends out his word, and melts them; he makes his wind blow and the waters flow. Psalm 147:15-18

See Matthew 8:18, 23-27; Mark 4:35-41; and Luke 8:22-25 where Jesus calms the storm.

Our days

The truth of God's sovereignty can remain a distant, ethereal idea – meaning, we think He's off handling only big issues and far removed from our everyday lives. Or we can personalize it and recognize His providence even in the things we think are small or trivial. Before the sun rose and set on the first day, your birthday and death-day were written in God's book. His sovereignty and foreknowledge extends to the lifespan of every human being who has and will ever live.

Your eyes saw my unformed substance; in your book were written, every one of them, the days that were formed for me, when as yet there was none of them. Psalm 139:16

See now that I, even I, am he, and there is no god beside me; I kill and I make alive; I wound and I heal; and there is none that can deliver out of my hand. Deuteronomy 32:39

…and the End

God is the beginning (Alpha), and He is the end (Omega). God is not reacting to world events. God is orchestrating them.

I am the Alpha and the Omega, the beginning and the end. Revelation 21:6

Remember this and stand firm, recall it to mind, you transgressors, remember the former things of old; for I am God, and there is no other; I am God, there is none like me, declaring the end from the beginning and from ancient times things not yet done, saying, "My counsel shall stand, and I will accomplish all my purpose," calling a bird of prey from the east, the man of my counsel from a far country. I have spoken, and I will bring it to pass; I have purposed, and I will do it. Isaiah 46:8-11

See also Isaiah 44:6; 48:5, 12.

We find stability and strength if, by faith, we accept that there is a God, who is all-powerful, all-knowing, and all-present. We grow in confidence that, despite popular opinions or how things look from where we stand, our world is not careening out of control. God actually does have the whole world in His hand. Resting in that reality, we aren't forced to try to save the planet, preserve the human race, or stare down the next existential threat. We know that God sits securely on His throne, ruling and reigning over every square inch of the universe. We have the peace of God that "surpasses all understanding" (Philippians 4:7) knowing that nothing happens that has not first come to His throne. God is the King of the universe.

Is it well?

In 1873, Horatio Spafford wrote the words of the beautiful hymn, "It is well with my soul." The story behind the hymn is tragic.

Spafford was a successful lawyer in Chicago. When the great Chicago fire destroyed the city, Spafford, like many others, suffered massive financial losses. Several years after the fire, with the city slowly recovering, Spafford decided to travel to Europe with his wife and four daughters for vacation. Because of some business issues, Spafford sent his wife Anna and their daughters ahead on the *S.S. Ville du Havre*, a ship bound for Wales. During the journey across the Atlantic, the ship sank and all of Spafford's daughters died. When his wife arrived in Wales, two simple words contained in the message conveyed the tragedy to Spafford, "Saved alone." When Spafford sailed to meet his wife, he wrote these words near the spot where his daughters had perished.

> When peace like a river attendeth my way,
> When sorrows like sea billows roll;
> Whatever my lot, thou hast taught me to say,
> It is well, it is well with my soul.

How can somebody face tragedy and loss and then write such profoundly beautiful words? How can faith in God remain? How can anyone after such loss say, "It is well with my soul"? And mean it? How can you? It is only by accepting, believing, and trusting in the truth that there are no such things as accidents or coincidences. God is in complete control. His sovereignty conveys His ownership. Spafford's daughters first and foremost belonged to God. This reality doesn't erase sorrow, but it does sustain us through it. Bible Commentator William Barclay wrote, "Sorrow can do one of two things to us. It can make us hard, bitter, resentful, rebellious against God. Or, it can make us kinder, softer, more sympathetic. It can despoil us of our faith. Or, it can root faith ever deeper and more immovable. It all depends how we think of God."[10]

Truth #1 challenges us to acknowledge the reality of God's sovereignty. By faith we believe that God is not absent, distant, or aloof. The Bible explains that God is ruling and reigning. So why would God sink a ship? He could have stopped it, so why didn't He? That brings us face to face with Truth #2 – All things exist for God's glory.

Prayer of confession and belief –

God, you are in complete control. As your servant Job prayed, so I pray too. You give and you take away, blessed be your name. Amen.

For further reading: Job 1-2; Psalm 57:2; Psalm 138:8; and 1 Samuel 2:6-8

Why, God? WHY WAS I ABUSE

HY, GOD?   Why, God?

ng won't   why don't you lov

Why do awful things happen?

WHY, GOD?   why does the Bib

HY, GOD? WHY, GOD?

OD? Why is this happening to

Y GOD?   W

why should I trust you, God?

things happen to innocent

WHY, GOD?

don't you   GOD yourself?   WHY, G

Y WON'T YOU ANSWER MY PRAYERS? WHY

WHY, GOD?   WHY,

Why doesn't God save everyone

hy did you create me, God?   GOD

is my life falling apa

Y DOES GOD LET BAD

Why, God? Why should I l

d you let this happen?

od? WHY AM I SO ANXIO

hy do bad things happen to go

WHY, GOD?

is there so much darkness?   wife get cancer?

TRUTH #2
ALL THINGS EXIST FOR GOD"S GLORY

"What is the chief end of man? To glorify God and enjoy him forever."[11]

– Westminster Shorter Catechism

Have you ever been told "Don't ask why - it's not our place"? I suppose that idea sounds like it's in the Bible, but it isn't. Knowing "the why" is important. Why am I doing this task? Why did the boss or management make this decision? Why did the national, state, or local government do or not do something…we want to know *why*!

In the Gospel of John, the disciples came to Jesus with a *why* question. While they were in Jerusalem, they noticed a beggar who was blind. With what seems like a slightly cruel curiosity, the disciples ask, "Rabbi, who sinned, this man or his parents, that he was born blind?" (John 9:2). During the time of Christ, when a child was born with a disability or stillborn or something tragic happened in someone's life, it was assumed that they had offended God somehow. Because of this culturally accepted falsehood, the disciples asked why, but their minds were limited to only two potential answers: either the parents sinned or the blind man sinned.

In certain cases, within our modern culture, we may be tempted to think the same way. We use words like karma or phrases like, "What goes around comes around," or a Bible verse, you reap what you sow (Galatians 6:7). Some people might even use super spiritual-sounding ideas like a family or generational curse to explain tragedy.

Jesus' response to the disciples' question deals a crushing blow to this erroneous and hurtful idea. "It was not that this man sinned, or his parents," Jesus responds (John 9:3). I can imagine the wheels in the disciples' heads started to turn. They felt safe in the assumption that all disabilities were a direct result of a specific offense against God. Then Jesus drops a bomb. The reason *this* man was born blind was "that the works of God might be displayed in him" (John 9:3).

In this particular story, Jesus makes some mud on the ground using His spit and He anoints the man's useless eyes with that mud. Jesus then instructs the man to go and wash in a nearby pool of water. In faith, having *not seen* but only hearing Jesus' voice and feeling his hands, he goes, washes, and instantaneously sees for the first time in his life. Jesus had given sight to this blind man.

A mix of wonder and skepticism follows. The man's parents are stunned. He actually has to convince other people that he used to be the blind beggar they supported. I imagine those conversations being quite humorous. But not everyone was celebrating. The religious leaders didn't care about a miraculous healing. They're just agitated with Jesus *again*. In this case, Jesus did a miracle on the Sabbath, a sacred religious day reserved for rest and worship.

The religious leaders quickly summon the formerly blind man for questioning. When first asked how this happened, he credits, "The man called Jesus" (John 9:11). Then a little bit later when asked his opinion about Jesus, he says, "He is a prophet" (John 9:17). Then when he stands before a religious tribunal, he says of Jesus, "Whether he is a sinner I do not know. One thing I do know, that though I was blind, now I see" (John 9:25). The evolution of his opinion about Jesus shows a growing faith. Here was a man who couldn't be educated because of his disability. A man who is viewed by the vast majority of the population as being punished by God. He isn't trying to engage in a theological debate. He is stating the facts as he *sees* them.

Outraged by this man's boldness and honesty, the religious leaders insult him and cast him out. "You were born in utter sin," they snidely say, "and would you teach us?" (John 9:34). This was more than just saying *get out of my office or out of my sight*. Because of his disability, the man had been excluded from the joys and privileges of other Jews. For just a few hours, he had been welcomed into the temple, but the religious leaders casting him out meant that he was just as excluded from the Jewish religious community as before. What a roller coaster of a day! Then Jesus finds him.

Keep in mind, the man has no idea what Jesus looks like. Here's the interaction the Apostle John records.

> Jesus heard that they had cast him out and having found him he said, "Do you believe in the Son of Man?" He answered, "And who is he, sir, that I may believe in him?" Jesus said to him, "You have seen him, and it is he who is speaking to you." He said, "Lord, I believe," and he worshiped him. John 9:35-38

In his mind, Jesus went from being simply a man, to a messenger from God, to a miracle worker, and finally Lord. Think for a moment: if he would have just received his sight, physically he would have been much better off. Spiritually though, he would still be blind. He would have tried, like so many others, to do good deeds to earn God's eternal favor. The restoration of sight would have given him the ability to learn a trade, find a wife, raise a family, and be a contributing member of society, but his spiritual blindness would have remained. Grace saved him from physical darkness, but he needed to be saved from the eternal darkness of

Hell (Matthew 8:12). Jesus did more than just give physical sight; He illuminated the man's spiritual eyes.

So why was he born blind? It wasn't something his parents or he had done wrong, but what God had done. God tells Moses in Exodus 4:11, "Who has made man's mouth? Who makes him mute, or deaf, or seeing, or blind? Is it not I, the Lord?" This man was born blind for the expressed purpose of bringing glory to God! And that glory was seen not just in the miracle of healing, but most powerfully in the man's salvation prayer, "Lord, I believe." Absolutely everything exists and happens for a reason. What reason? – God's glory.

Glory is about honor, splendor, and majesty. When an athlete wins a gold medal or a team wins a championship, they experience the glory of victory. Imagine an athlete or team winning and the trophy being handed over to the second or last-place team. It would be wrong. The glory of the gold medal belongs to the winner. They are placed on the highest platform and only their anthem is played. This is why worshiping and giving glory to other gods is so grievous to the one true God. He and He alone deserves the glory. The Bible calls this idolatry or spiritual adultery. Idolatry gives credit and honor that belongs only to God to another.

I am the Lord; that is my name; my glory I give to no other, nor my praise to carved idols. Isaiah 42:8

From the first pages of the Bible, the majesty of the Creator is the central theme. When Job encounters God, God begins with creation as a testament to His power and supremacy. God asks Job, the clearly rhetorical question, "Where were you when I laid the foundation of the earth?" (Job 38:4). Then He lets

Job in on a little secret. God recounts that while He was creating everything from nothing, "the morning stars sang together and all the angels shouted for joy" (Job 38:7, NLT). The angels, who are pretty spectacular themselves, seemed to be overwhelmed by the magnificence of God at work. These created beings weren't in awe of the creation, but the Creator. They responded by shouting for joy and singing songs of worship to God. They just couldn't hold back. They gave Him glory!

From the mighty angels of heaven to the smallest creature on earth, all of creation is made for the purpose of declaring the great glory of the Creator. Creation is a giant arrow pointing to the Creator.

The heavens declare the glory of God. Psalm 19:1

Holy, holy, holy is the Lord of hosts; the whole earth is full of his glory. Isaiah 6:3

Everyone who is called by my name, whom I created for my glory, whom I formed and made. Isaiah 43:7

For from him and through him and to him are all things. To him be glory forever. Amen. Romans 11:36

Yet for us, there is one God, the Father, from whom are all things and for whom we exist, and one Lord, Jesus Christ, through whom are all things and through whom we exist. 1 Corinthians 8:6

For by him all things were created, in heaven and on the earth, visible and invisible, whether thrones or dominions or rulers or authorities – all things were created through him and for him. Colossians 1:16

In every Bible story you've ever heard or read, it isn't man's glory or fame that's being celebrated or highlighted. These characters aren't the Christian version of comic book superheroes. The central theme and focus of each historical account in Scripture is God's glory, splendor, and majesty. Think about a few classics.

Abraham is the spiritual father of the faithful, but he began his life as an idol worshiper. God claims the glory for rescuing, blessing, leading, and providing many offspring for this saint.

> Long ago, your fathers lived beyond the Euphrates, Terah, the father of Abraham and of Nahor; and they served other gods. Then I took your father Abraham from beyond the River and led him through all the land of Canaan, and made his offspring many. Joshua 24:2-3

The Exodus isn't about Moses. It's all about God's glory.

> And I will harden the hearts of the Egyptians so that they shall go in after them, and I will get glory over Pharaoh and all his host, his chariots, and his horsemen. And the Egyptians shall know that I am the Lord, when I have gotten glory over Pharaoh, his chariots, and his horsemen. Exodus 14:17-18

> He saved them for his name's sake. Psalm 106:8

> For the scripture says to Pharaoh, "For this very purpose I have raised you up, that I might show my power in you,

and that my name might be proclaimed in all the earth."
Romans 9:17

David killing the giant Goliath isn't about a super-shepherd. It's about God winning the unwinnable battle for His people.

This day the Lord will deliver you into my hand.
1 Samuel 17:46

Shadrach, Meshach, and Abednego were three young Hebrews living in Babylonian captivity. They refused to bow down to a statue that was built to honor the king. As punishment, they were thrown into a blazing, fiery furnace. When they are rescued by the power of God, the violent King praises God.

Blessed be the God of Shadrach, Meshach, and Abednego...who trusted in him, and set aside the king's command, and yielded up their bodies rather than serve and worship any god except their own God. Therefore I make a decree: Any people, nation, or language that speaks anything against the God of Shadrach, Meshach, and Abednego shall be torn limb from limb, and their houses laid in ruins, for there is no other god who is able to rescue in this way. Daniel 3:28-29

In the same book of the Bible, Daniel was thrown into the lion's den. When God miraculously rescues Daniel, the new king makes a similar decree.

I make a decree, that in all my royal dominion people are to tremble and fear before the God of Daniel, for he is the living God, enduring forever; his kingdom shall never be destroyed, and his dominion shall be to the end. He delivers and rescues; he works signs and wonders in heaven and on earth, he who has saved Daniel from the power of the lions. Daniel 6:26-27

These last two stories aren't promises from God to always rescue His people. Throughout the centuries, lots of believers have been martyred by flames and lions. God didn't always shut the lion's mouths or make His people fireproof. In some cases, the greater glory given to God was in the death of His people.

Precious in the sight of the Lord is the death of his saints. Psalm 116:15

This he said to show by what kind of death he was to glorify God. John 21:19

God's grace of shepherding and caring for His people is for "his name's sake" (Psalm 23:1-3). God's mercy toward sinners in forgiving and forgetting sins, He says is "for my own sake" (Isaiah 43:25). God restrains His anger, "for the sake of my praise" (Isaiah 48:9).

This reality is not limited to just Bible stories. Your story and mine are part of the grand narrative of the glory of God. Even the trying and refining moments in our lives are for God's glory (Isaiah 48:10-11). All of history is *His* story. "God is for God."[12]

Does that make God an egomaniac?

If God is in sovereign control over the universe and made everything for the praise of His glory, does that make Him a maniacal, controlling narcissist? Is God an egomaniac? In the human mind, when we hear "God is for God" we might be tempted to accuse God of being and acting in sinfully, self-centered ways. But what if from the beginning God's glory and human happiness were essentially one and the same thing?

To answer that question we need to return to the biblical account of creation. God created Adam and Eve and placed them in a beautiful and bountiful garden. They were in perfect fellowship with their Creator. God had given them everything they needed, including each other. God had done this for His glory and for their joy and satisfaction. However, Satan soon assaulted the peace of the garden. At the foundation of his attack was the lie that God was keeping a higher level of happiness from humanity. The serpent said, "God knows that when you eat of it your eyes will be opened, and you will be like God" (Genesis 3:5). The serpent, Satan, had rejected fellowship with God and now he was enticing humanity to follow the same treacherous path. Tragically, Eve believed Satan and Adam followed suit. Their fellowship with God *and* their happiness were instantly destroyed.

Rebellion against God (sin) is believing happiness and fulfillment are found somewhere other than God. Saint Augustine writes, "You made us for yourself, and our hearts are restless, until they rest in you."[13] There is no higher joy, satisfaction, or pleasure than being in friendship with our creator. King David writes, "In your presence there is fullness of joy; at your right hand are pleasures forevermore" (Psalm 16:11). Like a loving parent wanting what is best for their children, God is offering what is best for us. And what is best for us is Him. Pastor John Piper often says, "God is most glorified in us when we are most satisfied in him."[14] God's glory and human happiness are inseparable.[15]

Even parts of your story or mine that are embarrassing or shameful or confusing or painful are part of God's glorious story and ultimately for our good. The Apostle Paul in Romans writes, "And we know that for those who love God all things work together for good, for those who are called according to his purpose" (Romans 8:28). Let me tell you a personal story about how I learned this truth.

God's Story for God's Glory

In 1959, Fidel Castro came to power in Cuba. Forty years later, I graduated from high school. Those two events happened many decades and miles apart, in two different countries, but they ended up being connected. During the summer of 1999 (by the way, so sick of hearing Prince's, "Party Like It's 1999"), I moved to Dallas to begin school at Dallas Baptist University (DBU). I was an 18-year-old kid, 1,200 miles from home. When I was in first and second grade, my family lived just outside of Dallas, so 10 years later, I had a few, vague recollections of people. One of them happened to be a lady who worked at DBU. My instructions were to fly to Dallas, get to campus, and find this lady's office. She was going to help me get registered. I had applied so late that the college had to call me to tell me I was accepted. The letter wouldn't have made it in time. I landed in Dallas, got to campus, and she was gone for the day. No joke, I had one check in my pocket to pay for the semester (all the money I had), a trunk, and a gigantic Rubbermaid container with all my stuff. I was standing in the library without a clue what to do next.

Within just a few moments, a lady named Deemie stepped out of her office and asked if she could help me. I had to have had a pretty helpless expression on my face, because from that day on Deemie and her family pretty much adopted me. A few weeks later, my maternal grandfather died. He was only 61. I flew back to Michigan for the funeral and then back to college. I returned to school alone and grieving. I was depressed and ready to drop out of school just one semester in. For the next three years, my parents made me go back to college, every single semester! I felt like God was punishing me, but He was writing a beautiful story.

In November of 2000, I put on a tuxedo and spoke at a college fundraiser to some super-rich Dallas folks. Senator Kay Bailey Hutchinson was the keynote speaker. I can't remember what I said, (the script was given to me) but it seemed to go well – so well that after the program I met Dr. Cook, the president of the university. We talked for a few moments and he asked me to come to his office the next day to talk. In my life when principals, deans, and college presidents ask for a meeting, it normally isn't a good thing. This meeting turned out quite different.

The next day I made my way across the campus to the president's office. I had never been in there. I was 19 years old and, looking back, I imagine I had on sandals, cargo shorts, and an orange DBU t-shirt. I hope I dressed better than that, but probably not. I sat down with the president of the university, for what would become another life-changing meeting. He asked me what I wanted to do with my life. I explained that I wanted to serve in pastoral ministry. I recall him telling me that he had been a pastor (which I remembered from my first week at school). Then he looked at me and told me I would never pay for school again. He was going to take care of it. To this day, I legitimately have no idea why he did that. I wasn't a great student. I was on academic probation most of the time. The idea of giving me a scholarship seemed outrageous.

Every semester following, I would register for classes, take my form to the cashier and sheepishly explain, "I don't know how this works, but Dr. Cook pays for my school." I would hand them the sheet and walk to my dorm to wait for a phone call telling me I was stupid and to get back to the cashier immediately and pay my tuition. The phone never rang. The president of the university was good to his word.

You'd think that I was happy, and I should have been, but the truth was I was broke, sinful, alone, angry, and depressed. I wanted to drop out, but my parents and an extremely generous scholarship wouldn't let me. God was in control and He was doing something for His glory that I couldn't see.

Jennifer and I got married in July of 2002. A few weeks later we moved to Texas so that I could finish school. I walked into Deemie's office and said, "I want to graduate in two semesters." She laughed. She explained to me that I hadn't taken any of my foreign language credits and that it would take me at least four semesters to finish. I registered for classes, really not having a clue how I was going to graduate the following May. A few days went by when Deemie called me. I remember her lovingly saying, "You are a spoiled brat. The community college down the road is offering fast-track Spanish – four semesters of Spanish in two. I've checked and it works perfectly with your schedule." Let's face it, I've been pretty spoiled.

I was going to spend five hours, Monday through Thursday, in Spanish. Jen and I went to the college bookstore to buy the book and noticed that the professor's name was the same as the author of the book. Instantly I was afraid. There was no turning back. I imagined a high and mighty professor who traveled between semesters, wrote books, and refused to stoop to helping students. And I had just signed up to spend nine months with this guy!

The first day of class came. I walked down a long flight of stairs to a classroom on the lower level. The walls were decorated with pictures and artifacts from Spanish-speaking countries. I took my seat and nervously waited. A few minutes later an energetic, kind man in his early 50's walked in. His name was Juan Baldor. We were instructed to call him Señor.

What transpired over the next nine months was something truly special. Señor and I became friends. Not in the sucking-up-to-your-professor way, but genuinely, we connected as people. I invited Señor to our church for special programs. We went to lunch and visited some antique shops together. Jen and I shared dinners with him and his wife, Beth. It was during that time that I learned that Juan and his family had fled Cuba as Castro was taking over the country. As a young immigrant, he had learned English by watching cartoons in Miami. Eventually, he and his family moved to Dallas. When I met Juan Baldor, I wasn't super Gospel/evangelism-minded, but something happened with me and Señor that changed us both.

I did graduate in two semesters. We celebrated with a wonderful dinner with family and friends. It was an academic and financial miracle. Part of me is still waiting for the university to call and explain that there was a big mistake and they want my degree back and some money! After graduation, Jen and I packed up our little apartment and moved back to Michigan.

Señor and I on graduation day - May 16, 2003.

Señor and I stayed connected. I found myself in Dallas a few times over the next couple of years. I remember Deemie calling me and asking me about Juan. She explained that DBU was looking for a Spanish teacher and that because of my experience with Juan, they wanted to hire him. What I didn't know is what God had done and was doing in Señor's life. He had gotten saved. He had given his life to Christ. He soon retired from the community college and served for the next 10 years at DBU. He is retired from teaching now, but he serves in his church, translates materials in Spanish for mission work, and has gone on several mission trips. He recently messaged me, saying that he was in Guatemala and shared "our story."

Hindsight may not be 20/20, but some things certainly become clearer over time. When I felt miserable, alone, depressed, and wished to be anywhere but at school, God was doing something I couldn't see and wouldn't understand for years. Why did God take me and keep me at DBU? The answer is Juan Baldor. It all started with the frustration of the lady I was supposed to see being out of the office, Deemie to Dr. Cook, to Juan Baldor, and back again. I still shake my head in disbelief. I was a 21-year-old know-it-all who really knew nothing at all, who God used.

Forty years before I graduated high school, a little boy and his family fled their home in Cuba. He ended up in Dallas and so did I. He offered fast-track Spanish, and I needed to graduate. Matter of fact, it's the only time in his career he ever offered fast-track Spanish. Why? Because God was going to use me so that *He* could rescue and save Señor. God was writing "our story." It's a story that began in another country long before I was even born! It's an epic, God authored story that brings Him glory and brings me great joy.

Señor wrote me a letter in August 2019. Here is a small excerpt:

> Josh, you know that He used you to open my eyes and my heart to Him. He used you to lead me to be born again, as I have surrendered my life to Him and I have been truly transformed. I realize that I am a sinner and fall short, but I live every day to serve Him, to bring Him glory…

Who gets the glory? God. Who feels joy? Señor and me.

The reformers had a set of core beliefs that we call the Solas. Soli Deo Gloria was a Latin phrase that was both a doctrine and greeting of sorts. It means Glory to God alone. When it comes to Juan Baldor…*Soli Deo Gloria*. Or better yet in Spanish, Gloria solo a Dios.

Until…

You might be thinking okay, so God is in control and all things exist for God's glory, but really, how does God get glory out of suffering or disasters or trials or calamity? It can be easy to see how God gets glory from a story of blessing and victory. Even God's glory in the beauty of creation, a magnificent piece of art, or music makes sense. But suffering? How does God get glory out of that? Doesn't that seem cruel and even sadistic?

When we think about this mystery, we are asking a fairly logical question: Why do bad things happen to good people? And at the same time, we are asking the question: Why do good things happen to bad people? Even the Psalmist wrestled through this confusion. He laments:

> Behold, these are the wicked; always at ease, they increase in riches. All in vain have I kept my heart clean and washed my hands in innocence. For all the day long I have been stricken and rebuked every morning. If I had said, "I will speak thus," I would have betrayed the generation of your children. But when I thought how to understand this, it seemed a wearisome task, until I went into the sanctuary of God; then I discerned their end. Psalm 73:12-17

Asaph, the writer, looked around and saw his own suffering compared to the prosperity of the wicked. He didn't understand.

As He tried to reconcile this reality, the puzzle seemed to just grow more complex and confusing. I love the word "until." On his own he tried to make sense of his circumstances, but failed...*until* he went to God. Then he discerned. He realized the eternal judgment that is waiting for the wicked. He celebrates in his circumstance that God holds his right hand (vs. 23), guides him (vs. 24), promises to receive him into glory (vs. 25), strengthens his heart (vs. 26), and provides refuge in time of trouble (vs. 28).

Like Asaph, we can try to understand this reality on our own and grow exhausted and weary. Or we can have that "until" moment where we go to God and see Truth #3 – God's ways are not our ways.

Prayer of confession and belief –

God, like a deer pants for water, my soul is thirsty for you. All that has been created is for your glory. I rejoice to know that I have been made for a high and holy purpose. I am thrilled to know that you are most glorified when I am most satisfied in you.[16] And when I am satisfied in you, I am at my most joyous. Your glory and my joy are inseparable. First your glory, then my joy. Thank you Lord. Amen.

For further reading: Psalm 37:4; Psalm 42:1-2; Psalm 63:1-2; 2 Chronicles 20:12

WHY, GOD? WHY WAS I ABUSE

HY, GOD? WHY, God?

hy won't why don't you lov

Why do awful things happen?

WHY, GOD? why does the Bib

HY, GOD? WHY, GOD?

OD? Why is this happening to r

Y GOD? W

HY, GOD? why should I trust you, God?

things happen to innocent

Why, GOD?

don't you show yourself? WHY, G

Y WON'T YOU ANSWER MY PRAYERS? WHY

WHY, GOD? WHY,

why doesn't God save everyone

hy did you create me, God? GOD

is my life falling apa

TY DOES GOD LET BAD

Why, God Why should I

d you let this happen?

od? WHY AM I SO ANXIOU

why do bad things happen to go

WHY, GOD?

is there so much darkness? wife get cancer?

TRUTH #3
GOD"S WAYS ARE NOT OUR WAYS

"God moves in a mysterious way."[17]

- William Cowper, poet and hymn writer

When we encounter the God of the Bible, we realize He declares Himself to be all-powerful (omnipotent), all-present (omnipresent), and all-knowing (omniscient). In stark contrast, we are none of those things. Accurately understanding God is the only way to gain a correct understanding of ourselves. The Old Testament Prophet Isaiah "saw the Lord sitting upon a throne, high and lifted up" (Isaiah 6:1). It was during a difficult year of national change as the long-time king, Uzziah, died. When Isaiah sees the Lord, his first response is, "Woe is me! For I am lost; for I am a man of unclean lips, and I dwell in the midst of a people of unclean lips; for my eyes have seen the King, the Lord of hosts" (Isaiah 6:5). For both Job and Isaiah, God's majesty went well beyond their limited mental, physical, and spiritual perspective.

Both the Bible and our common human experience teach us that we are far from all-powerful, all-present, or all-knowing. We each must face the limits of our mental and physical abilities. All of humanity is constrained by time and space. We can only be in one place and in one moment at a time. The proverb is true: Time waits for no man. God, by stark contrast, is outside of time, space, and unencumbered by any inability. C.S. Lewis writes, "In God you come up against something which is in every respect immeasurably superior to yourself. Unless you know God as that – and, therefore, know yourself as nothing in comparison – you do not know God at all."[18]

Simply stated: there is a God and we are *not* him. His abilities and ways are unique only to Him and, as we'll see, radically different than our own.

For my thoughts are not your thoughts, neither are your ways my ways, declares the Lord. For as the heavens are higher than the earth, so are my ways higher than your ways and my thoughts than your thoughts. Isaiah 55:8-9

Can you find out the deep things of God? Can you find out the limit of the Almighty? It is higher than heaven – what can you do? Deeper than Sheol – what can you know? Its measure is longer than the earth and broader than the sea. Job 11:7-9

God's way is holy.

I will remember the deeds of the Lord; yes, I will remember your wonders of old. I will ponder all your work, and meditate on your mighty deeds. Your way, O God, is holy. Psalm 77:11-13

God's way is everlasting.

The counsel of the Lord stands forever, the plans of his heart to all generations. Psalm 33:11

God's thoughts are wise.

Oh, the depth of the riches and wisdom and knowledge of God! How unsearchable are his judgments and how inscrutable his ways! For who has known the mind of the Lord, or who has been his counselor? Romans 11:33-34

God's ways are beyond critique.

> Behold, God is exalted in his power; who is a teacher like him? Who has prescribed for him his way, or who can say, "You have done wrong?" Job 36:22-23

God's view is heavenly.

> Be not rash with your mouth, nor let your heart be hasty to utter a word before God, for God is in heaven and you are on earth. Therefore let your words be few. Ecclesiastes 5:2

God's power is supernatural.

> As you do not know the way the spirit comes to the bones in the womb of a woman with child, so you do not know the work of God who makes everything. Ecclesiastes 11:5

Our Ways

Humanity is the polar opposite. Not only in our abilities and inabilities, but our values and views are completely different from God. Arthur Pink accurately writes, "Much of the contents of the Bible conflicts with the sentiments of the carnal mind, which is enmity against God."[19] Our way isn't just opposite; our way is opposed to God's way. The Apostle Paul writes that the fallen mind "is hostile to God" (Romans 8:7). Songs from every recent generation and genre declare, essentially, it is my life and I'll do what I want with it. In our own poetry, we defy God by claiming to be "the master of [our] fate...the captain of [our] soul."[20] In his letter to the Romans, Paul summarizes what direction we steer our own souls.

"None is righteous, no, not one; no one understands; no one seeks for God. All have turned aside; together they have become worthless; no one does good, not even one." "Their throat is an open grave; they use their tongues to deceive." "The venom of asps is under their lips." "Their mouth is full of curses and bitterness." "Their feet are swift to shed blood; in their paths are ruin and misery, and the way of peace they have not known." "There is no fear of God before their eyes." Romans 3:10-18

That's a definitive, comprehensive view of humanity's spiritual condition. God is holy, we are anything but. Our ways are earthly, foolish, disobedient, rebellious, and broken. And on top of all of that, we are dirt. Psalm 103:14 says, "We are dust." We are both earthly and earthy. King Solomon writes, "There is a way that seems right to a man, but its end is the way to death" (Proverbs 14:12).

The following illustration falls ridiculously short of capturing the poetic beauty of the prophet Isaiah's phrase, "As the heavens are higher than the earth, so are my ways higher than your ways," (Isaiah 55:9), so please forgive me. Every parent has a perspective that their children lack. Experience has given them wisdom and, in some cases, a better point of view. When a child is young, the warnings may be about crossing the street or strangers or electricity. As a child grows, the warnings change. They may revolve around relationships, money, jobs, driving, social media, or other issues of which the parent has a more mature perspective. Using this simple idea, God is the parent and we are the child. His view is greater, higher, and wiser. We are limited, shortsighted, stubborn, rash, and often reckless. God is God and we are not.

But what if we were God, just for a moment? Let's imagine you or I get to be God for a day.

God for a Day

In the early 2000's, a movie came out exploring this idea. The movie titled *Bruce Almighty* stars Jim Carrey as a man given God's power for a week. I can't recommend the movie, but the story is somewhat honest. At first, Carrey's character uses his on-loan powers for selfish purposes. One particular divine "duty" the title character is assigned is the answering of prayers. He decides to answer all prayers with an automatic "yes" just so he can avoid the work. When the pressure of divinity grows too great, Bruce realizes he needs and wants God to be God.

Let me make this clear – we aren't, we can't be, and, contrary to certain religions, we never will be God (gods, goddesses, or one of the gods). This is purely an imaginative exercise, but for the sake of an illustration – what if you were God? What if I was God? Holiness would be out the window! Like Bruce, I would use this borrowed power for selfish purposes. Oh, and lots of smiting! Anyone who has ever offended me, lied about me, stole from me, or hurt me...smitten! As a matter of fact, anyone who does evil also smitten! Oh wait, I just smote (is that correct grammar?) the whole world. I wouldn't be a god who is "merciful and gracious, slow to anger, and abounding in steadfast love and faithfulness" (Exodus 34:6). My rigid personality would probably lead to judgment all the time!

Maybe you'd be a more loving god? You are naturally softer and nicer than me. You'd forgive everybody for everything because you're just a super nice, gracious deity. No judgment – just love! I suppose you'd be viewed as kind and benevolent. But what happens to the victims when you forgive all the villains? Are they just supposed to get over their abuse? You would inadvertently create a world with zero justice – no consequences for any evil or wrong. What about just eliminating the concept of evil altogether? Oh wait, we just by default abolished good as well. With this train of thought we find ourselves in an untenable, philosophical quandary.

Maybe you'd be a god who was more human, more in the moment. Eventually, that would lead to the human default of being moody, inconsistent, and unpredictable. You might paint beautiful sunrises and sunsets one day and the next bury Miami in a snowstorm. "Power corrupts; absolute power corrupts absolutely."[21] What would divine power do?

We need God to be God. And thankfully, God is not a man.

> I will not execute my burning anger; I will not again destroy Ephraim; for I am God and not a man, the Holy One in your midst, and I will not come in wrath. Hosea 11:9

We are not God and God is not like us. God's ways are not our ways. Our vantage point leaves us stuck in the present, moving minute by minute into the future, completely unable to change the past or control what's coming. On the other hand, God controls the future. And although He doesn't change the past, He can fix it. Or to use an important word from the Bible - He *redeems* it.

Joseph and the Redeemer

Included in the Old Testament book of Genesis is one of the more dramatic and puzzling stories in the Bible. The storyline centers around Joseph, the favorite son of the patriarch Jacob (later named Israel). The mix of Jacob's favoritism, Joseph's immaturity, and the brother's jealousy was a powder keg. Joseph's brothers grew to hate him so much that they collectively decided to murder him. This wasn't isolated sibling rivalry. Just the sight of this young man infuriated them. One day as Joseph approached them, instead of murder, they changed their minds and decided to sell him into slavery. In some ways, this fate could be viewed as worse than death. Psalm 105:18 says that Joseph's "feet were hurt with fetters; his neck was put in a collar of iron." Little did they know that their treachery was all part of God's plan. The brothers returned home to their father with a fabricated story about Joseph being killed by a wild beast. Joseph was now a slave far from his father and his home. The journey took him to Egypt, prison, and eventually by God's providence Joseph became second in charge of all of Egypt. It's a miraculous turn of events. (For the full story read Genesis chapters 37, 39-50 – a one paragraph summary does not do justice to this saga.)

As the years go by, Joseph's brothers are forced by a famine to come to Egypt for food. Who do they encounter? Joseph! He's in charge of the sale and distribution of food. It's a phenomenal setup for the best revenge story ever! But God's ways had become Joseph's ways. He does not ignore or excuse their sin against him. Look what he says:

I am your brother, Joseph, whom you sold into Egypt. And now do not be distressed or angry with yourselves because you sold me here, for God sent me before you to preserve life...And God sent me before you to preserve for you a remnant on earth, and to keep alive for you many survivors. So it was not you who sent me here, but God. Genesis 45:4-5, 7-8

Later in the story, as the family had been reunited and saved from starvation, together they mourned the death of their father Jacob. This caused great anxiety and fear in Joseph's brothers. They assumed because Jacob was gone, Joseph's revenge would now be unleashed. Read Joseph's startling words:

Do not fear, for am I in the place of God? As for you, you meant evil against me, but God meant it for good, to bring it about that many people should be kept alive, as they are today. Genesis 50:19-20

In the account of Joseph, God's complete control and glory is on display. However, God's way of accomplishing this beautiful, compelling, transformative, and joyous journey was long, methodical, and, at times, unclear. Eventually, Joseph recognized that God was the author of the whole story. God was the hero, not Joseph. God got the glory, not Joseph. And God got the glory in *His* way. Every confusing twist and turn had been divinely designed. Humanly-speaking, Joseph's story seems like a perfect set up for *revenge*. Divinely speaking, Joseph's story is an awesome example of *redemption*. It is one of many illustrations that highlight a really important part of God's character. God's ways are the ways of the Great Redeemer.

In the Old Testament, a redeemer was a person of important cultural significance. When a relative was murdered, it was up to the nearest relative to seek retribution. This person was called a redeemer. When a man died, his closest single relative would marry the widow. This was called redeeming. A redeemer was one who would buy back property that a relative sold in distress. He would redeem what had been lost. A redeemer had the noble task of avenging, delivering, ransoming, and restoring. Job, the suffering servant of God, in great faith proclaimed, "For I know that my Redeemer lives, and at the last he will stand upon the earth" (Job 19:25).

God is *the* Redeemer. He restores what has been broken. He finds what has been lost. He gives justice to the abused. He ransoms the captives. He buys back what has been stolen. He removes the shame of the grieving, lonely widow. In Joseph, God redeemed his suffering to bring salvation.

Does it have to be suffering?

Why does *the* Redeemer so often use suffering and trials? Why not sunshine and roses? Because success doesn't sanctify. We want ease, but ease never produces righteousness. Suffering does. The Psalmist writes, "Before I was afflicted I went astray…It is good for me that I was afflicted, that I might learn your statutes…in faithfulness you have afflicted me" (Psalm 119:67, 71, 75). In the depths of his suffering Job cries out, "Though he slay me, yet will I trust in him" (Job 13:15, KJV).

In one of his letters to the church at Corinth, Paul clues us in to his own suffering. He writes:

So to keep me from becoming conceited because of the surpassing greatness of the revelations, a thorn was given me in the flesh, a messenger of Satan to harass me, to keep me from becoming conceited. Three times I pleaded with the Lord about this, that it should leave me. But he said to me, "My grace is sufficient for you, for my power is made perfect in weakness." Therefore I will boast all the more gladly of my weaknesses, so that the power of Christ may rest upon me. For the sake of Christ, then, I am content with weaknesses, insults, hardships, persecutions, and calamities. For when I am weak, then I am strong. 2 Corinthians 12:7-10

I am so glad we don't know what Paul's thorn in the flesh was, because this biblical promise isn't limited to oppressive people or bad eyesight or some other specific difficulty. God's promise to preserve His people through all suffering is the guarantee to redeem all forms of trials or trouble we may face. Paul reveals the central purpose in his suffering and suffering for all time. God takes His children to a school[22] of suffering to keep us from becoming self-reliant. Chuck Swindoll, one of the great preachers and writers of our time, sees God's way of inflicting suffering as the Lord removing all our crutches that we by default rely on rather than trusting and depending on God.[23]

"God will never give you more than you can handle," is a pithy, Bible-sounding statement that a lot of well-meaning Christians give as encouragement, but it is *not* true. God will give you more than you can handle, so that you will stop relying on your own strength, resources, connections, plans, schemes, and ideas! Paul writes in that same letter to the Corinthian church:

For we do not want you to be unaware, brothers, of the affliction we experienced in Asia. For we were so utterly burdened beyond our strength that we despaired of life itself. Indeed, we felt that we had received the sentence of death. But that was to make us rely not on ourselves but on God who raises the dead. He delivered us from such deadly peril, and he will deliver us. On him we have set our hope that he will deliver us again. 2 Corinthians 1:8-10

Paul even goes so far as to say, "We rejoice in our sufferings" (Romans 5:3). James writes, "Count it all joy, my brothers, when you meet trials of various kinds, for you know that the testing of your faith produces steadfastness. And let steadfastness have its full effect, that you may be perfect and complete, lacking in nothing" (James 1:2-4). Those thoughts are completely contrary to the way our human minds think. We want God to conform to our ways, rather than conforming our ways and thoughts to His. The Apostle was seeing and understanding things God's way.

Suffering, trials, difficulties, and wounds are God's gracious way of training. The Bible says, "He wounds, but he binds up; he shatters, but his hands heal" (Job 5:18). When God wants to write a great story that displays His glory, He breaks a man or woman. He deeply wounds them. If He doesn't, we'll hijack His glory. We'll grab the trophy. We will take credit, accept the accolades, and revel in the praise. In our fallen state, we want the glory because that's *our way*! And God's way isn't our way.

We as humans love to achieve, because then we can accept some or all of the credit. God's ways of grace are not about achieving but receiving. We receive grace and mercy. And because we received and didn't achieve, God gets the glory. Paul received grace from God to endure during this trial. We must be trained by suffering. We must be baptized in anguish[24] before we truly see our fallen ways and the glorious ways of God.

Redeemed

Think about the stories from the Bible we have seen so far. Each person suffered tremendously because that is God's way. Then and only then can there be REDEMPTION! People see the redeemed and then they look for *the* Redeemer! God gets the glory His way!

The blind man from John chapter 9 – REDEEMED!

Years of struggling with his disability left his survival to the mercy of people walking by. He was likely only able to eat because of people's pity and charity. In the end he believes, worships, and *sees* Jesus face to face!

Job, the suffering servant – REDEEMED!

Job's story ends with the words, "And the Lord blessed the latter days of Job more than his beginning" (Job 42:12). Job's story began with God calling him His servant and ends with God calling Job "my servant" (Job 42:7). Suffering didn't change Job's standing with God, but it did change the servant. For the first time, he saw who God truly was.

Joseph – REDEEMED!

He seems to have been a disrespectful, entitled brat. When the story ends, he says, "Am I God, that I can punish you? You intended to harm me, but God intended it all for good. He brought me to this position so I could save the lives of many people" (Genesis 50:19-20, NLT).

The Apostle Paul – REDEEMED!

Even in his trials, Paul proclaims, "The sufferings of this present time are not worth comparing with the glory that is to be revealed to us" (Romans 8:18). Then in his final letter, with the glory of victory in sight, he tells Timothy, "I have fought the good fight, I have finished the race, I have kept the faith. Henceforth there is laid up for me the crown of righteousness, which the Lord, the righteous judge, will award to me on that day" (2 Timothy 4:7-8).

All of their suffering, trials, and difficulties were redeemed. They were given meaning and purpose. God never wastes pain. He never inflicts more than is necessary. It is supremely for His glory, but also for our good! In the book titled *The Great Divorce*, C.S. Lewis writes, "This is what mortals misunderstand. They say of some temporal suffering, 'No future bliss can make up for it,' not knowing that Heaven, once attained, will work backward and turn even that agony into a glory."[25] Moses writes, "Make us glad for as many days as you have afflicted us, and for as many years as we have seen evil" (Psalm 90:15). Through the prophet Joel, God says, "I will restore to you the years that the swarming locust has eaten, the hopper, the destroyer, and the cutter, my great army, which I sent among you" (Joel 2:25). God doesn't change the past, but He does redeem, restore, and renew.

I have seen this. Crisis leads us to the Lord in a way that a life of ease never would. A few years ago, a young couple named Mike and Cindy showed up to our church. They were expecting their first child. We had mutual friends, so we connected quickly. A few months went by and I got a phone call that this couple, well into their third trimester, had miscarried. I raced to the hospital. I'll never forget the frightened look on Cindy's face. I watched Mike care so deeply for his wife, but there was nothing we could do but pray. Later that day, Cindy gave birth to a stillborn baby girl named Ira.

A few days later I was asked to do a small memorial for Ira with some family and friends. I walked up a long driveway, not really knowing what to expect. We gathered by a little pond. I opened the Bible and tried to say something coherent. When I left, I wept as I walked to my car. I remember looking to God like, "Really?" I was so confused. They had just started to really seek the Lord and now this! I recall thinking, "Well, I'll never see them again."

My way wasn't God's way. I thought God messed up, but He didn't. I have seen God redeem what I thought to be unredeemable. Years later, Mike and Cindy were blessed with a beautiful boy and then twins. We've celebrated salvations and baptisms. It all started from that beautiful little girl named Ira. Her name means "watchful." I guess that's the message. I was wrong. God was right and He was going to let me *watch* His redeeming plan unfold.

When I first talked to Russell that day in 2017, I stopped here. I only had three truths to share. As I recall, Russell pointed out that something was missing. He was right. Yes, God is in complete control. Yes, all things exist for God's glory. And most certainly, God's ways are not our ways. But these three realities alone leave us with a God who is all-powerful and purposeful, but impersonal. That brings us to the final and most tender truth…

God loves us. That's right. God loves you. God loves me.

Prayer of confession and belief –

God, your way is not my way. My way leads to destruction, chaos, and pain. From this day forth, when I make plans, I will stamp them all with "Lord willing." "If the Lord wills, [I] will live and do this or that." Your way is higher. I trust your way. I submit my plans and my way to your sovereignty, for your glory and my joy. Amen.

For further reading: Genesis 37, 39-50; Psalm 105:16-24; Psalm 107; Jeremiah 29:11

Why, God? WHY WAS I ABUSE
HY, GOD? Why, God?
hy won't why don't you lov
Why do awful things happen?
WHY, GOD? why does the Bib
HY, GOD? WHY, GOD? WH
OD? Why is this happening to
Y GOD?
why should I trust you, God?
things happen to innocent
WHY, GOD?
don't you show yourself?
WHY, G
Y WON'T YOU ANSWER MY PRAYERS? WHY
WHY
VHY, GOD? Why doesn't God save everyone
hy did you create me, God? GOD
is my life falling apa
TY DOES GOD LET BAD
Why, God? Why should I
d you let this happen?
od? WHY AM I SO ANXIO
why do bad things happen to go
WHY, GOD?
is there so much darkness?
wife get cancer?

TRUTH #4
GOD LOVES YOU

"God loves each one of us as if there were only one of us to love."[26]

– Saint Augustine, pastor, theologian, and philosopher

God loves you – just pause and think about that. The very God who is right now ruling and reigning over every square inch of the universe knows you (Matthew 10:30) and loves you. God who created the stars, planets, and solar system for His glory, also uniquely created you (Psalm 139:13-17). The One whose ways are higher than ours is redeeming all things for His glory and offering Himself to us for our eternal joy. But life is hard. We may know in our head that God has a plan, but struggles and disappointments can leave us asking in our heart, "Does God really love *me*?"

As God introduces Himself in the Old Testament, God says He is "abounding in steadfast love" (Exodus 34:6). David writes, "Your steadfast love is better than life" (Psalm 63:3). Psalm 119:64 says, "The earth, O Lord, is full of your steadfast love." Does God love you? The answer is a resounding "Yes!"

In 1 John 4:7-8, the Apostle called the beloved writes, "Let us love one another, for love is from God, and whoever loves has been born of God and knows God. Anyone who does not love does not know God, because God is love." Is God only love? Of course not. But the very concept of love is introduced into creation by God. Love is part of the essence of God's character. Eternity, moral absolutes, and creation all point us to the Creator. So does love. We know love because it comes from God. As we understand true love (1 Corinthians 13:4-7), we catch a greater glimpse of who God is.

As humans, we can be quite flippant with love. We fall in and out of love. We feel love, or we feel nothing, and therefore, love must be gone. Love can be used to manipulate and control. Our version of love is often cheap, a thing of convenience. It is self-serving. Our broken hearts pervert love. God's way purifies and preserves true love. John writes, "We love because he first loved us" (1 John 4:19).

"But this or that doesn't feel loving," you may say. The reason we think this way or perceive certain actions from God as unloving is because our definition of love is broken. We have to let God define love. Because our way of loving is fallen and earthly, it produces flawed expectations. God's ways are higher than ours, and that includes His way of loving. God truly does love you and He shows it in an extravagant, out of this world way.

God showed how much he loved us by sending his one and only Son into the world so that we might have eternal life through him. 1 John 4:9 (NLT)

Like any great affection, love needs action. It needs to be demonstrated. It needs to be proved. Evangelist Billy Graham was known for often saying, "God proved His love on the Cross. When Christ hung, and bled, and died, it was God saying to the world, 'I love you.'"[27] The proof of God's love for you is found at the cross.

For God so loved the world, that he gave his only Son, that whoever believes in him should not perish but have eternal life. John 3:16

You and I are included in the world! It's the word cosmos. Nobody is excluded from the infinite, steadfast love of God. Now, because of our pride, we may be tempted to respond to such a truth with, "Of course...I'm pretty lovable!" But that isn't the case at all. Each person is immensely valuable, but that's not the same as being lovable.

The Imago Dei and The Fall

From the very beginning, humanity has been created in the image of God. On the first page of the Bible, the book of Genesis says, "God created man in his own image, in the image of God he created him; male and female he created them" (Genesis 1:27). We call that the Imago Dei - meaning every person born, both men and women, are an image bearer of the Creator. At the core, that means every person is valuable and worthy of dignity and respect; not for what we do or a particular group we belong to, but because of the very essence of our being. There is nothing that a person can do that erases the stamp of their Creator. As God's image bearers, we are the ambassadors and representatives of *the Creator*. We have been given dominion over God's good creation. What an amazing reality that it is that we bear the image of God, but are we lovable in our nature and actions? The honest and objective answer is "no."

The magnificence of the Genesis story in chapters one and two takes a terrible turn in chapter three. We fall. We rebel. God had placed humanity in a beautiful garden. He had provided food, human relationships, and ultimately Himself. But we rejected that truth for a lie. Adam and Eve betrayed God's kindness. They broke the one restriction God had given them. They ate of the Tree of Knowledge of Good and Evil. Adam sinned against God and, as a representative of all humanity, he led the human race into sinful rebellion against the Creator. Because of sin, God curses Adam, Eve, and all of future humanity. These amateur sinners quickly became pros. In the next few chapters of human history, we see jealousy, murder, lying, revenge, polygamy, wickedness, and nearly worldwide destruction.

From the garden on, we have all lived in a fallen, broken world. Are physical trials and suffering by divine decree or a natural consequence of our fallen world? The answer is "yes," it's a both/and. How we each are uniquely affected by the Fall of Genesis chapter 3 is sovereignly determined by God. The Fall has a unique physical, emotional, social, mental, and spiritual impact on each person. This is what Romans 8:22 means, when the Apostle Paul writes, "That the whole creation has been groaning together." The groan is because we, and all of creation, have been captured and are waiting to be rescued (redemption – Romans 8:18-25).

Paul on several occasions summarizes the effect of the Fall on humanity, and it isn't pretty. "For we ourselves," Paul writes, "were once foolish, disobedient, led astray, slaves to various passions and pleasures, passing our days in malice and envy, hated by others and hating one another" (Titus 3:3). The reality for fallen humanity is that in and of ourselves, we are far from loving or lovable. We have a serious problem – sin. We weren't in the garden, but Adam led humanity's rebellion against God and we have joyfully followed suit. If you have any doubts about that, the 10 Commandments provide conclusive proof.

You shall have no other gods before me.

You shall not make for yourself a carved image, or any likeness of anything that is in heaven above, or that is in the earth beneath, or that is in the water under the earth. You shall not bow down to them or serve them…

You shall not take the name of the LORD your God in vain, for the LORD will not hold him guiltless who takes his name in vain.

Remember the Sabbath day, to keep it holy. Six days you shall labor, and do all your work, but the seventh day is a Sabbath to the LORD your God.

Honor your father and your mother.

You shall not murder.

You shall not commit adultery.

You shall not steal.

You shall not bear false witness against your neighbor.

You shall not covet your neighbor's house; you shall not covet your neighbor's wife, or his male servant, or his female servant, or his ox, or his donkey, or anything that is your neighbor's.

Exodus 20:2-17

We have all broken these commandments, time and time again (Romans 3:23). Even on the commandment of murder, there's no escaping on a technicality. In teaching on this specific commandment, Jesus said, "Everyone who is angry with his brother will be liable to judgment; whoever insults his brother will be liable to the council; and whoever says, 'You fool!' will be liable to the hell of fire" (Matthew 5:22). Later the Apostle John echoes Jesus' teaching. He writes, "Everyone who hates his brother is a murderer" (1 John 3:15). We are 0 for 10, so we stand guilty before God (James 2:10).

We are sinners by nature and by choice. Romans 6:23 says, "The wages of sin is death." The penalty for sin has always been death. God declared that all the way back in the Garden of Eden. That is bad news. Actually, it's compoundingly bad news. The consequences of sin do include physical death, but also what the Bible calls the second death – and it's much worse than the first.

The second death is a place of God's unrelenting judgment and wrath against sin. This place is a place of eternal suffering called Hell. The Gospels describe Hell as a place of "outer darkness," "weeping and gnashing of teeth," "eternal fire prepared for the devil," "eternal punishment," "torment," and "anguish" (Matthew 25:30; 25:41, 46; Luke 16:23-24). With God, it's His way or the highway. That wide, multi-lane highway does, in fact, lead to Hell. Even Hell burns eternally to the glory of God.

We need to let that sink in for a moment. That is really *bad* news. But this *bad* news paves the way for the really, really *good* news. Good news that we call the Gospel.

God shows His love for us in that while we were still sinners, Christ died for us. Romans 5:8

While we were at our worst, most broken, rebellious, sinful, godless state of living – God demonstrated, displayed, and proved His LOVE for us at the cross. CHRIST DIED FOR US! There at the cross, our sin and rebellion collided with the unmatched love, mercy, and salvation of God! Seven hundred years before Jesus Christ would die on the cross, the Old Testament prophet Isaiah, wrote of the suffering Savior:

He was despised and rejected by men, a man of sorrows and acquainted with grief; and as one from whom men hide their faces he was despised, and we esteemed him not. Surely he has borne our griefs and carried our sorrows; yet we esteemed him stricken, smitten by God, and afflicted. But he was pierced for our transgressions; he was crushed for our iniquities; upon him was the chastisement that brought us peace, and with his wounds we are healed. All we like sheep have gone astray; we have turned–every one–to his own way; and the LORD has laid on him the iniquity of us all. He was oppressed, and he was afflicted, yet he opened not his mouth; like a lamb that is led to the slaughter, and like a sheep that before its shearers is silent, so he opened not his mouth. By oppression and judgment he was taken away; and as for his generation, who considered that he was cut off out of the land of the living, stricken for the transgression of my people? And they made his grave with the wicked and with a rich man in his death, although he had done no violence, and there was no deceit in his mouth. Isaiah 53:3-9

Just reading that passage of Scripture leaves me in awe of the love and mercy of God. We, like rebellious sheep, went our own way, but God laid the punishment for our sin on Jesus. At the Cross of Calvary, God was displaying His love, mercy, and power as never before. Jesus willingly laid down His life to pay the penalty for sin. Nobody forced Him (John 10:17-18).

Greater love has no one than this, that someone lay down his life for his friends. John 15:13

After his death, Jesus was quickly buried in the borrowed tomb of a rich man named Joseph of Arimathea. Jesus did die to pay for sin, but He rose from the dead. After Jesus's resurrection, His students walked and talked with Him, ate with Him, listened to Him teach, touched Him, worshiped Him, and watched Him gloriously ascend into Heaven (Acts 1:9). These disciples wrote down their first-hand, eyewitness accounts of Jesus rising from the dead!

The Bible declares Jesus as King, ruling and reigning on the throne of Heaven. This great King loves you. Through His work on the cross and subsequent resurrection, He has made a way for us to be saved from our sin. We must repent of our sin and believe in the death and resurrection of Jesus. Romans 10:9 says, "If you confess with your mouth that Jesus is Lord and believe in your heart that God raised him from the dead, you will be saved." This is *the* good news. This is *the* one and only Gospel. Nothing more *and* nothing less. Turn from sin and believe the Gospel (Mark 1:15).

If you do, you will be pardoned from the eternal consequences of your sins, that is called justification. You will immediately have a right standing before God. You will be given the gift of eternal life – that is called glorification. Death will no longer be a terror to you, but an exit from the temporal struggles of this earth and entrance into the eternal, everlasting presence of God (2 Corinthians 5:6-8). Between the moment of justification and the future hope of glorification is the promise of God's comforting presence in your life. This is called sanctification. Justification, sanctification, and glorification are each made possible because of the extravagant love of God demonstrated through the death and triumphant resurrection of His only son Jesus.

Mary, Martha, and Lazarus

In the Gospel of John, we are introduced to a special family that Jesus became friends with. Mary, Martha, and Lazarus lived in a little village called Bethany, which was just a couple of miles outside of Jerusalem. It seems from several biblical stories that Jesus spent significant time with these siblings. I think it was likely that when the Lord traveled to Jerusalem for Jewish holidays, He stayed in Bethany at Martha's house with His disciples.

In John chapter 11, a message is sent to Jesus that Lazarus is really sick. It was a sickness that was so serious it warranted getting word to Jesus right away. The message was simple, "Lord, he whom you love is ill" (John 11:3). Jesus was a renowned miracle worker. Surely Mary, Martha, and Lazarus' connection with and hospitality to this famous rabbi had earned them a healing. Jesus' response is quite unexpected and strange. Here's what the Apostle John records:

> When Jesus heard it he said, "This illness does not lead to death. It is for the glory of God, so that the Son of God may be glorified through it." Now Jesus loved Martha and her sister and Lazarus. *So*… (John 11:4-5, italics added for emphasis)

They loved Jesus. Jesus loved them. Lazarus was sick and Jesus healed sick people. "So…" you would expect that the loving, miracle-working Jesus would have canceled His plans and immediately made His way back to Bethany. But that isn't what happened. John records, "When He heard that Lazarus was ill, he stayed two days longer in the place where he was" (John 11:6).

After the sisters sent word to Jesus, I picture them waiting with great anticipation for the Lord's arrival. But day after day, hour after hour as their brother grew weaker, Jesus was nowhere to be found. I imagine Mary and Martha thinking during those long days, "Where is Jesus? I thought He loved my brother? I thought He loved *me*?" And then, Lazarus died.

Four days later, Jesus and His disciples arrived in Bethany. When Martha finally sees Christ, she seems to give Him a piece of her mind. "Lord," she says, "if you had been here, my brother would not have died" (John 11:21). A little later, Mary falls at the feet of Jesus and says the same thing. They were friends with a miracle worker and they desperately needed His help, but Jesus didn't show up in time. They were heartbroken and grief stricken. Their faith was shaken, because Jesus had failed to meet their expectations.

Like Mary and Martha, we often link God's love with our expectations. When God "fails" to meet our expectations, we might question His love for us. In those moments we must let truth trump our feelings.

> For as high as the heavens are above the earth, so great is his steadfast love toward those who fear him. Psalm 103:11

> For your steadfast love is great above the heavens. Psalm 108:4

> "For the mountains may depart and the hills be removed, but my steadfast love shall not depart from you, and my

covenant of peace shall not be removed," says the Lord, who has compassion on you. Isaiah 54:10

I have loved you with an everlasting love. Jeremiah 31:3

Jesus really loved Lazarus, so why didn't He heal him? In the gospels Jesus had actually done miracles across great distances without even being present with the person. He certainly could have done that for Lazarus, but He didn't. Why? Because Jesus was going to show Martha, Mary, *and* Lazarus more than a miracle.

The Lord traveled to the tomb where His friend was buried and there He wept. The crowds of people commented, "See how he loved him!" (John 11:36). Christ's love for Lazarus was evident in the tears that He shed and His power would be unmistakable in what He did next. Jesus called Lazarus by name and raised him from the dead. News of this miracle would spread throughout the entire region. Jesus had brought a dead man back to life!

What happened at Lazarus' tomb wasn't just an incredible miracle, it was a preview of something greater. Christ's death and resurrection showed that His power *and* His love are both limitless! With Christ, death is not the end. Eternal life is made possible by the love of God! This is the hope that Mary, Martha, Lazarus, and the disciples were given that day in Bethany. A.W. Tozer writes, "...because God is self-existent, His love had no beginning; because He is eternal, His love can have no end; because He is infinite, it has no limit; because He is holy, it is the quintessence of all spotless purity; because He is immense, His love is an incomprehensibly vast, bottomless, shoreless sea before which we kneel in joyful silence and from which the loftiest eloquence retreats confused and abashed."[28]

When we believe in Jesus (John 11:25), we are confident that in every season of life we are a recipient of God's steadfast, unchanging love. Christ is the declaration of God's love to the world. Jesus is also *the* definitive proof that God understands and empathizes with our suffering and sorrow. Being loved by God doesn't mean an easy, pain-free life. God does not promise to eliminate struggles, but He does vow to go through them with us. His presence is what provides perseverance through the pain. God says, "I will never leave you nor forsake you" (Hebrews 13:5). When God professes His love, He promises His presence.

My wife, Jennifer, found this beautiful poem and shared it with me. She has shared it with some of our friends who are mentioned in this book.

> Pain knocked at my door and said she'd come to stay.
> Though I would not welcome her but bade her go away,
> Still she entered —
> And like my shade she followed after me,
> And from her stabbing stinging sword
> No moment was I free.
> And then one day another knocked most gently at my door.
> I cried, "No! Pain is living here; there's no room for more."
> And then I heard His tender voice, "'Tis I, be not afraid."
> And from that day He entered in – the difference that it made!

For though He did not bid her leave — my strange unwelcome guest,
He taught me how to live with her;
And no one ever guessed that we could dwell so sweetly here –
My Lord, and pain and I – within this fragile house of clay,
While years slip slowly by.[29]

God recognizes that grief is not something you get over, but something you go through. He promises to go through it with you. One of my favorite song lyrics simply says, "Sometimes he calms the storm, and other times he calms his child."[30] Christ walks through the storms of life with us. He stands right with us as a seemingly endless amount of waves crash against us. He stands in the fire with us. He is near to the brokenhearted (Psalm 34:18). We do not have to fear what is coming, because He is with us. He will strengthen and help us. And when we don't feel like we can stand, He says, "I will uphold you with my righteous right hand" (Isaiah 41:10).

In difficult and challenging circumstances, we can be confident in our loving, heavenly Father's power, purpose, and providence! God is in complete control. All that happens exists for His glory. His ways are not our ways. And what makes us embrace these truths is God's loving embrace of us. The glory of His power is equally matched by the majesty and magnificence of His love for you and me.

Prayer of confession and belief –

God, thank you for creating me and loving me. I confess that I have rebelled against you. I have broken your laws. But in your kindness, you have made a way for me to escape the eternal consequences of my sins. I repent of my sin and turn to you as Lord and Master of my life. I believe that you died and rose again from the grave. I stand in awe that you know everything about my past, present, and future and still without any hesitation profess your love for me. I give you praise and glory. Amen.

For Further reading: John 3:16; Romans 3:23; 5:8; 6:23; 10:9, 13; Psalm 136

Why, God? WHY WAS I ABUSE
HY, GOD? Why, God?
hy won't why don't you lov
Why do awful things happen?
WHY, GOD? why does the Bib
HY, GOD? WHY, GOD? WH
OD? Why is this happening to
GOD?
HY why should I trust you, God?
GOD? things happen to innocent
WHY, GOD?
don't you kill yourself?
WHY G
WHY,
Y WON'T YOU ANSWER MY PRAYERS? WHY
HY, GOD? why doesn't God save everyone
hy did you create me, God? GOD
is my life falling apa
Y DOES GOD LET BAD
Why, God? Why should I
d you let this happen?
od? WHY AM I SO ANXIO
hy do bad things happen to go
WHY, GOD?
is there so much darkness?
my wife get cancer?

JESUS AND THE FOUR MOST IMPORTANT TRUTHS

"The cross is the center of the world's history; the incarnation of Christ and the crucifixion of our Lord are the pivot round which all the events of the ages revolve. The testimony of Christ was the spirit of prophecy, and the growing power of Jesus is the spirit of history."[31]

– Alexander MacLaren, Scottish Pastor

Christ is the divine intersection of the four most important truths. The life, death, and resurrection of Jesus is the time and space where all four truths collide. Jesus died on the cross by the definite plan of God, to the glory of God, in a way that baffled the disciples and all of humanity, demonstrating the awe-inspiring, matchless love of God for lost sinners - sinners like you and me.

God is in complete control

The arrest, trial, and execution of Jesus Christ was not a haphazard event. The chaos of the crowd, the vengeful religious leaders, and a scrambling Roman prefect (Pontius Pilot) were all part of God's sovereign plan to provide salvation for sinners. The Apostle Peter in his sermon on the day of Pentecost, calls it, "the definite plan…of God" (Acts 2:23). The crucifixion of Christ wasn't an inconvenient plot twist that God was forced to respond to. This was God's design from before the very foundation of the world. God wasn't a helpless spectator. He was masterfully directing every element — including the betrayal of His only begotten Son.

Judas Iscariot has gone down in history as the man who betrayed his friend, Jesus, for 30 pieces of silver. He's become the archetype for betrayal. Judas was a man chosen to spend three years learning from the Lord Jesus. He seems to have been one of the more trusted disciples because he was in charge of the money (John 12:6). Yet, he was a thief and appears to have only followed Jesus with financial and political aspirations as his motive. When Judas came to the realization that Jesus wasn't going to conquer Roman tyranny and establish Himself as the ruling Jewish king, the disillusioned disciple looked for an opportunity to cash out. The religious leaders of the day were eager to contract Judas because they wanted to quietly arrest Jesus and bring Him to a swift, violent end.

On the night of the Passover celebration, Jesus confided to His disciples that He knew one of them was plotting to betray Him. The identity of the traitor, Jesus said, "is he to whom I will give this morsel of bread when I have dipped it" (John 13:26). Jesus dipped the bread and handed it to Judas who was within reach. Judas became the fulfillment of the prophetic words in Psalm 41:9, "Even my close friend in whom I trusted, who ate my bread, has lifted his heel against me." Jesus affirms that specific prophetic fulfillment in John 13:18. As Judas accepted the bread, Satan himself possessed this "son of destruction." Jesus said to him, "What you are going to do, do quickly" (John 13:27). Hours later when Judas led a mob to the private praying spot of Jesus, Matthew 26:50 records the Lord saying, "Friend, do what you came to do." Luke 22:48 records Jesus asking him, "Judas, would you betray the Son of Man with a kiss?" Clearly, Judas was acting of his own volition, but legitimately possessed by Satan! That must garner some mercy from the readers and hearers of his tragic tale. But trumping Satan's vile intentions and Judas' sinful choice, God was orchestrating the whole unfolding story.

While Judas illustrates the paradox of God's sovereignty and man's responsibility, Jesus Christ literally embodies it. On that same night, Jesus prayed three times in the Garden of Gethsemane, "My Father, if it be possible, let this cup pass from me; nevertheless, not as I will, but as you will" (Matthew 26:39). Jesus is the God-Man – fully God and fully man. In the hours before His crucifixion, Jesus was submitting His human will to the divine. What a mystery the incarnation (God in the flesh) is!

The sovereignty of God and the free-will of man are both illustrated in the Gethsemane prayer. They are also clearly stated throughout the Scripture. How we reconcile these two seemingly incompatible ideas has been the source of endless debate. As a simple illustration, visualize these two concepts as separate and distinct lines. When lines intersect, they create a cross. And that is where God's sovereignty and man's free-will intersect — at the cross of Jesus Christ. They are made compatible within the God-Man. Jesus had a human will, but willingly submitted His will to the plan of God. The cross of Christ is where the seemingly opposite doctrines of God's Sovereignty and humanity's free-will harmonize.

What about us? What about free-will? Are we just robots? Puppets? A.W. Tozer writes, "God sovereignly decreed that man should be free to exercise moral choice, and man from the beginning has fulfilled that decree by making his choice between good and evil."[32] We exist within the paradox, the mystery (Deuteronomy 29:29). God *is* in complete control and we, like Christ, must submit our human will to the divine. We must have our own Garden of Gethsemane moment where we pray, "Thy will be done" (Matthew 26:42, KJV).

All things exist for God's glory

We have yet to straight out answer the age-old question: Why do bad things happen to good people? Before I answer, we need to first examine the question. To start – who gets to define what is good and what is bad? How do we determine who is good and who is bad? Jesus told a rich, young seeker, "No one is good except God" (Mark 10:18). About humanity, David writes, "There is none who does good" (Psalm 14:1). Nobody qualifies as good, because "all have sinned" (Romans 3:23). The question, then, is fundamentally flawed.

Why do bad things happen to good people? Actually, that's only happened once in history. A bad thing happened to the only *good* human to ever walk the planet – Jesus. At Calvary, He would face, not just nails, whips, spears, and ridicule, but the holy wrath of God for sin would be poured out on Him. God "made him to be sin who knew no sin, so that in him we might become the righteousness of God" (2 Corinthians 5:21). It was the plan of God that something "bad" happen to someone who was good, so that something good could happen to someone who was truly bad (Isaiah 53:10). This was all done for the glory of God.

Though he was in the form of God, did not count equality with God a thing to be grasped, but emptied himself, by taking the form of a servant, being born in the likeness of men. And being found in human form, he humbled himself by becoming obedient to the point of death, even death on a cross. Therefore God has highly exalted him and bestowed on him the name that is above every name, so that at the name of Jesus every knee should bow, in heaven and on earth and under the earth, and every tongue confess that Jesus Christ is Lord, to the glory of God the Father. Philippians 2:6-11

The sacrificial death of Jesus, the good God-Man, was all about God's glory! Christ's glorious work brought about the salvation of sinners, which increases the glory given to God. Jesus' substitutionary death would bring "many children into glory" (Hebrews 2:10, NLT). There it is – God's glory and our salvation (joy) paired once again.

God's ways are not our ways

The cross was once an emblem of Roman tyranny and terror, but has now become the symbol of the Christian life. On the surface that doesn't make a lot of sense. It seems dark and foreboding, like choosing an electric chair or noose as a symbol for a movement. The fact that God took the most horrific instrument of human execution and reclaimed it for His purposes shows that His ways are not our ways. While some see the cross as foolish, the Scripture says the cross "is the power of God" (1 Corinthians 1:18). This is the divine paradox of the Gospel – death is the door to life.

Then Jesus told his disciples, "If anyone would come after me, let him deny himself and take up his cross and follow me. For whoever would save his life will lose it, but whoever loses his life for my sake will find it." Matthew 16:24-25

The Son of God died on a Roman cross and then called His students to carry their own cross. Jesus challenged His followers to live a cruciform life – a cross-shaped life. A person molded by the cross surrenders complete ownership to divine purposes. Taking up our cross means continually toppling the kingdom of self and crowning Jesus as Lord. The Apostle Paul writes, "I die daily" (1 Corinthians 15:31, NASB). That perpetual dying is the only way to the newness of life that Jesus promises. It is the only way to peace with God. The cross is the only way to find meaning and purpose in our lives.

Sometimes people will use the phrase, "That's my cross to bear." In some ways they are right. The cross is a model for how to suffer well. Even though Christ is God's beloved son, Hebrews says, "He learned obedience through what he suffered" (Hebrews 5:8). Christ was not exempt from God's school of suffering. Like Jesus, we learn greater dependance and obedience to the Father as we take up our cross. We can joyfully embrace whatever cross we have to carry, because we are confident in Christ's proven, resurrection power![33]

Joining Jesus in death means we will also join Him in victory. The gruesome death of Jesus was followed with His triumphant resurrection from the dead. That is God's way: first trials *then* triumph – death and *then* resurrection.

God loves us

Imagine a timeline of human history stretching from the beginning until now. The cross of Christ stands at the very center. It is there that through Christ, God was providing "salvation to everyone who believes" (Romans 1:16). The visual in my mind is seeing Jesus' arms stretched out on the cross. One arm is reaching back into history and saving those who looked forward in faith to a coming Savior. The other arm is reaching through time to you, me, and even into the future to those of faith who will look back in time at the cross for salvation.

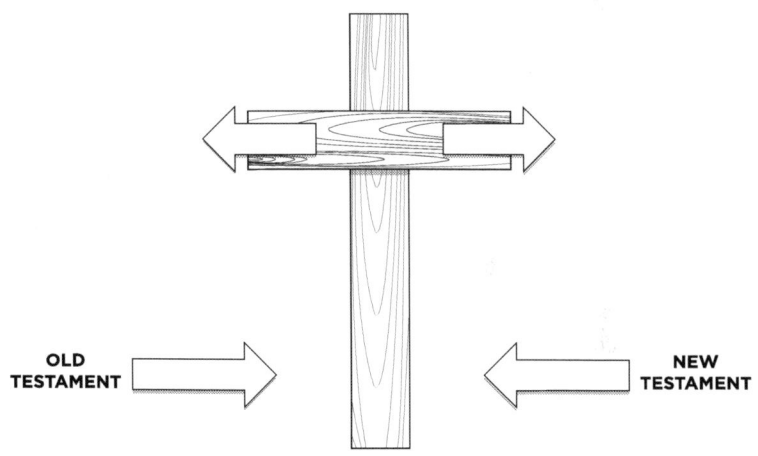

When we repent and believe in Jesus, we are welcomed by the love of God into a community. That community is the family of God. The saints of the Old Testament looked forward to the coming of the promised Messiah. The New Testament believers and those after them, look back to Christ. What unites us is the work of Christ on the cross. God's love brings this super-eclectic group together across time and space. His love leaps through history and across cultural, racial, national boundaries, and language barriers. His love makes a family out of *us* and *them*. John records in Revelation 7:9-10 the great family reunion in Heaven. He writes:

> After this I looked, and behold, a great multitude that no one could number, from every nation, from all tribes and peoples and languages, standing before the throne and before the Lamb, clothed in white robes, with palm branches in their hands, and crying out with a loud voice, "Salvation belongs to our God who sits on the throne, and to the Lamb!"

All four truths culminate in Christ. From the very beginning God has been in complete control, writing the story of His glory in a way that is unique, only to Him. Yet, God is not distant, but near. He is not aloof, but aware. He knows us and loves us. Christ is the proof that God is in control, working out all things for His glory and our good, and accomplishing His loving purposes in a mysterious, unexpected way.

Prayer of confession and belief –

God, when I reflect on the ministry and mission of Christ, I am in greater awe of who you are. That you would, from before the foundation of the world, have this plan in your heart leaves me speechless. I praise you for your sovereign, glorious, mysterious, and loving way.
Amen.

For further reading: 2 Corinthians 4:7-18; 1 Peter 2:21-25; 5:10-11

Why, God? WHY WAS I ABUSE
HY, GOD? Why, God?
ng won't why don't you lov
Why do awful things happen?
WHY, GOD? why does the Bib
HY, GOD? WHY, GOD? WHY
OD? Why is this happening to
Y GOD?
why should I trust you, God?
HY, GOD?
things happen to innocent
WHY, GOD?
don't you show yourself?
WHY G
Y WON'T YOU ANSWER MY PRAYERS? WHY
WHY, GOD? WHY
Why doesn't God save everyone
hy did you create me, God? GOD
is my life falling apa
TY DOES GOD LET BAD
Why, God? Why should I
d you let this happen
od? WHY AM I SO ANXIO
hy do bad things happen to go
WHY, GOD?
is there so much darkness?
wife get cancer?

WHY? GOD!

"God is too good to be unkind and He is too wise to be mistaken. And when we cannot trace His hand, we must trust His heart."[34]

– Charles Spurgeon

A few weeks after our lunch that spring day in 2017, Russell called and I instantly knew something was wrong. He was crying as he asked me to come to the hospital to dedicate his daughter to the Lord. I put on my purple and pink "Team Adalyn" shirt and drove to Ann Arbor. Though I've worn a few team jerseys in my life, none of them have meant as much to me as that purple shirt that I still treasure. As I gathered with family, friends, a mom, and a dad around a beautiful little girl, I couldn't hold back my tears. Truthfully, I can't remember what I said.

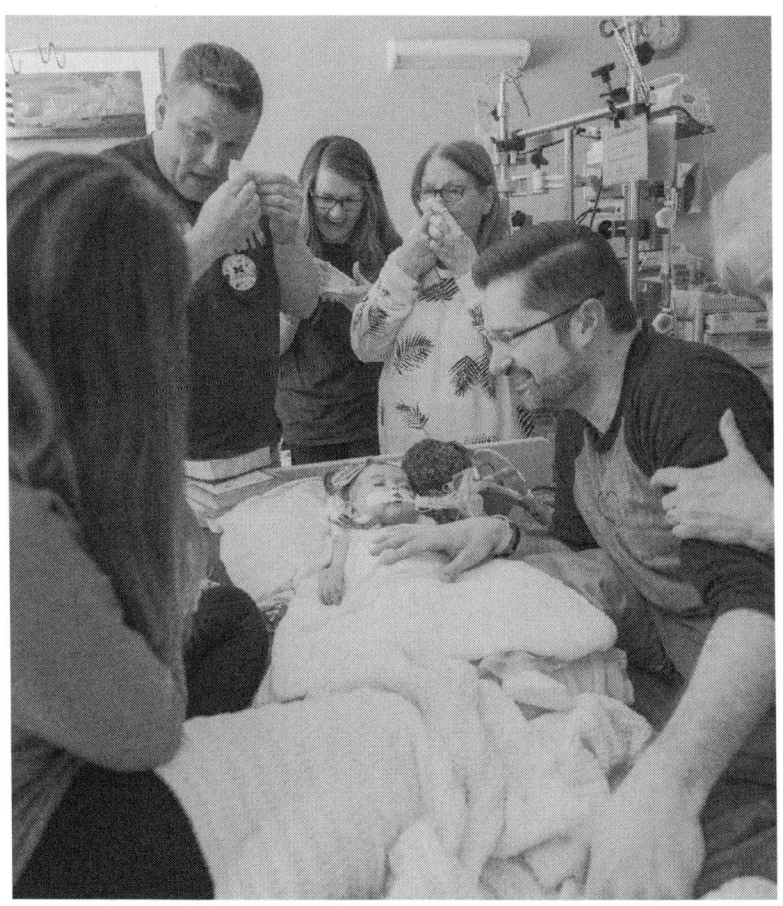

A short time later, she was gone. On May 18, 2017, Adalyn went to Heaven. We prayed and knew the best medical team around had done everything in their power to save her life.

The very next day, a precious man in our church was killed in a tractor accident. When I got that call, I could barely catch my breath. The weight of these two devastating deaths crushed me. I vividly recall sitting on a small hill near my driveway and weeping. I cried out to God. I was hurting, but I knew that people I loved were hurting so much more. As a pastor, I have felt pain for my dear flock and they have, at times, felt the deep hurt of their shepherd. The Apostle Paul writes, "If one member suffers, all suffer together" (1 Corinthians 12:26).

The man who was killed in the farm accident was an important man. In my mind and in my plan, he was absolutely necessary. I had met him four years earlier when his 38-year-old son, Raymond, had died from cancer. During that funeral, Raymond's two-year-old son, just being a toddler, escaped his caregiver and raced into the service. He ran down the aisle and attempted to pull himself up at the casket. The room froze in horror. He called out, "Daddy! Daddy!" Only by the grace of God, I calmly walked over and lifted him up. We talked about his dad. For the next few minutes, I held him while I continued preaching. It's a moment in my life that I will never forget.

Now four years later, God had taken his grandfather. How could this be good for that little boy? I wanted to give God a lecture on how this was a terrible plan. This wasn't fair. I drove to his grandmother's house, where the smell of a roast cooking filled the room. During our visit, Sue realized her husband Sonny would never be coming home to eat it.

On May 23, 2017, I did Adalyn's funeral. My wife Jennifer came and met Heather, Adalyn's Mom, for the first time. My wife unleashed her mama-bear. She cared for and fiercely protected Heather. I'll never forget traveling to a cemetery near where I grew up for the burial. The casket and the vault were so small. They shouldn't have to make those things that small – ever. Jen and I still talk about how hard it was for Heather and Russell to walk away from that grave.

The next year, God blessed my friends with another daughter. Imagine if Cindy-Lou Who were to step out of the pages of Dr. Suess. That's this girl. Instead of calling me Mr. Josh or Pastor Josh, she mashes them together and calls me Master Josh. Like her sister, she melts my heart.

A couple of years after that, they were expecting another daughter, but this would be where my faith would run into a brick wall. The day before Heather was to be induced, the baby died. Jen and I drove to the same hospital in Ann Arbor, Michigan. I was angry, confused, and felt totally helpless.

It was the summer of 2020. COVID-19 had overtaken the world. We masked up and went into the room. Even writing this, I have a hard time reliving those moments. The cruelty was that Heather would still have to deliver, but joy wouldn't follow. I was so overcome by emotion, I couldn't even speak. My wife, Jennifer, prayed. She boldly asked God to raise that sweet baby from the dead. She told God that we wanted to celebrate this child and not mourn her loss. We were pleading with God to do the miraculous, but He didn't.

A few days later on one of the hottest days of the year (it was 94 degrees when we started), Jennifer and I stood in that same cemetery we were in three years earlier. This time, I was left with little to say. What do you say to a father and mother who have lost two daughters? According to doctors, they had hit the genetic lottery twice. I was looking at the same grief-stricken faces. Nobody said it out loud, but in my own heart I heard the questions, "What now preacher? Where is God? Why did God let this happen *again*?"

I opened my Bible to the story of Jacob in Genesis 32:22-32. It is a story of an Old Testament saint and scoundrel literally wrestling with God all night. The story is strange, but it was what I felt like God was telling me to say. I encouraged my friends, actually I begged them, to keep wrestling with God through the darkness of their grief. I prayed they would hold on to Jesus even when things didn't make sense. I pray the same thing for you.

In the Gospel of Mark, a father in crisis cries out to Jesus, "I believe; help my unbelief" (Mark 9:24). He was confused *and* confident. He was hopeless *and* hopeful. It's hard to understand how both faith and unbelief can exist in the same heart at the same time. But that's the nature of our broken hearts and that is what we bring to God. The Apostle Peter encourages us to cast all of our fears and anxieties on Jesus, "because he cares for you" (1 Peter 5:7). "If you need wisdom," James writes, "ask our generous God, and he will give it to you. He will not rebuke you for asking" (James 1:5, NLT). We bring our hurt to the healer. We bring our confusion to the source of all wisdom. We bring our questions to *the* Answer. When life doesn't make sense, we can be certain of the four unchanging truths.

Why, God? WHY WAS I ABUSE

HY, GOD? Why, God?

hg won't why don't you lov

Why do awful things happen?

WHY, GOD? why does the Bib

HY, GOD? WHY, GOD? WH

OD? Why is this happening to

Y GOD?

why should I trust you, God?

things happen to innocent

don't you show yourself?

WHY, GOD?

WHY G

Y WON'T YOU ANSWER MY PRAYERS? WHY

WHY

VHY, GOD?

Why doesn't God save everyone

hy did you create me, God? WHY, GOD

is my life falling apa

Y DOES GOD LET BAD

Why, God? Why should I

d you let this happen?

od? WHY AM I SO ANXIO

hy do bad things happen to go

WHY, GOD? so much darkness?

is there so much wife get cancer?

EPILOGUE

In April 2018, I was headed down to Orlando for a unique speaking opportunity. I was essentially serving as a chaplain/motivational speaker (all I can picture is Chris Farley on *SNL*) for a mission team serving at *Give Kids the World*. If you are unfamiliar with this place, it is quite remarkable. It is a resort specially designed for families with children who have a life-threatening or terminal illness. It's a beautiful place, but it's also a place of deep pain.

As I prayed through how to equip the team with what to feel and, when given the opportunity, what to say, I came back to the four truths. The challenge of making these concepts memorable and transferable was a bit daunting, but I had an idea. In our modern culture of text, we have our own version of hieroglyphics. We just call them emojis. I searched through my iPhone to find four symbols that could help communicate and remind the team of these truths. Here's what I used.

💪 God is in Complete Control

🔼 All Things Exist for God's Glory

✳️ God's Ways Are Not My Ways

🖤 God Loves Me

I called a friend and had them printed on a simple bracelet. The response was incredible. What started with a life-changing conversation became a bracelet designed to help equip a mission team. Now, years later, a book. My hope is that you'll read the book and wear the bracelet. Not for some branding nonsense, but because I believe we need a daily reminder of who God truly is.

Why, God? WHY WAS I ABUSE

HY, GOD? Why, God?

hy won't why don't you lov

Why do awful things happen?

WHY, GOD? why does the Bib

HY, GOD? WHY, GOD? WHY

OD? Why is this happening to

Y GOD?

why should I trust you, God?

WHY, GOD?

things happen to innocent

WHY, GOD?

don't you show yourself? WHY G

Y WON'T YOU ANSWER MY PRAYERS? WHY

WHY, GOD? WHY,

why doesn't God save everyone GOD

hy did you create me, God?

is my life falling apa

Y DOES GOD LET BAD

Why, God? Why should I

d you let this happen?

od? WHY AM I SO ANXIO

hy do bad things happen to go

WHY, GOD?

is there so much darkness?

wife get cancer?

STUDY GUIDES

For deeper study, write down the ways you see each of the "4 Truths" demonstrated in the life of the biblical character from the provided passage of Scripture.

ABRAHAM
Genesis 11:27-25:18

God is in complete control:

_____

_____

_____

_____

_____

All things exist for God's glory:

_____

_____

_____

_____

_____

God's ways are not our ways:

_____

_____

_____

_____

_____

God loves us:

_____

_____

_____

_____

_____

MOSES
Exodus 1-19

God is in complete control:

_____
_____
_____
_____
_____

All things exist for God's glory:

_____
_____
_____
_____
_____

God's ways are not our ways:

_____
_____
_____
_____
_____

God loves us:

_____
_____
_____
_____
_____

DAVID
1 Samuel 16; 2 Samuel 2

God is in complete control:

_____

_____

_____

_____

_____

All things exist for God's glory:

_____

_____

_____

_____

_____

God's ways are not our ways:

_____

_____

_____

_____

_____

God loves us:

_____

_____

_____

_____

_____

RUTH
The Book of Ruth

God is in complete control:

_____
_____
_____
_____
_____

All things exist for God's glory:

_____
_____
_____
_____
_____

God's ways are not our ways:

_____
_____
_____
_____
_____

God loves us:

_____
_____
_____
_____
_____

ESTHER
The Book of Esther

God is in complete control:

_____

_____

_____

_____

_____

All things exist for God's glory:

_____

_____

_____

_____

_____

God's ways are not our ways:

_____

_____

_____

_____

_____

God loves us:

_____

_____

_____

_____

_____

PAUL

Acts 8:54-9:30; 2 Corinthians 11:21-12:10; Galatians 1:11-2:10; Philippians 3:4-11

God is in complete control:

_____
_____
_____
_____
_____

All things exist for God's glory:

_____
_____
_____
_____
_____

God's ways are not our ways:

_____
_____
_____
_____
_____

God loves us:

_____
_____
_____
_____
_____

YOU

Now, take a moment to reflect on the ways you see each of the "4 Truths" demonstrated in YOUR life.

God is in complete control:

_____
_____
_____
_____
_____

All things exist for God's glory: 1 Corinthians 10:31; Psalm 115:1

_____
_____
_____
_____
_____

God's ways are not our ways:

_____
_____
_____
_____
_____

God loves us:

_____
_____
_____
_____

Why, God? WHY WAS I ABUSE

HY, GOD? Why, God?

hy won't why don't you lov

Why do awful things happen?

WHY, GOD? why does the Bib

HY, GOD? WHY, GOD? WH

OD? Why is this happening to

GOD?

why should I trust you, God?

things happen to innocent

WHY, GOD?

don't you show yourself?

WHY, G

Y WON'T YOU ANSWER MY PRAYERS? WHY

WHY, GOD?

WHY

Why doesn't God save everyone

GOD

hy did you create me, God?

is my life falling apa

Y DOES GOD LET BAD

Why, God? Why should I

d you let this happen

od? WHY AM I SO ANXIO

why do bad things happen to go

WHY, GOD?

is there so much darkness? wife get cancer?

ACKNOWLEDGEMENTS

From the bottom of my heart, I want to thank Russell and Heather West, Mike and Cindy McCollum, Marcy, Riley, and Sue Doughty, and others who generously allowed me to use their stories. I am forever indebted to each of you. Thank you, Adalyn. God used you to change my life. I'm happy to be on your team. I can't wait to see you and your sister, Maelyn, in Heaven.

Thank you to my friends who helped make this project a reality. They read and re-read sloppy words that I vomited on a page and pretended to be a book: Sam Woodbeck, Amy Grimes, Tim Walter, Terri Kowalczyk, Michelle Nuckolls, and Donna Fox. A special thank you to Chuck Lindsey for reading specifically for theological content and creating the illustrations in chapter five.

Thank you to The River Publishing team: Randy "Doc" Johnson, Jeannie Yates, Michael J. Fox, Lorena Haber, and Shawna Johnson. Also, a thank you to Jill Osmon, the assistant to the elder team.

To my children, Claire-Anne, Belle-Anne, Maverick, Ruby-Sue, and Mavis: thank you for bringing food, coffee, and snacks to the study when I was writing.

Thank you to my wife, Jennifer-Anne, who for years encouraged and prodded me to get this done. You are my crown! (Proverbs 12:4)

Thank you Jesus for being so long-suffering with me. Your grace and kindness have led me to repentance. You are in control, for your glory, in a way that is for my good, because you love me!

Why, God? WHY WAS I ABUSE

HY, GOD? Why, God?

ng won't why don't you lov

Why do awful things happen?

WHY, GOD? why does the Bib

HY, GOD? WHY, GOD? WH

OD? Why is this happening to

Y GOD? W

why should I trust you, God?

HY things happen to innocent

WHY, GOD?

don't you show yourself?

WHY G

Y WON'T YOU ANSWER MY PRAYERS? WHY

HY, GOD? WHY,

why doesn't God save everyone

hy did you create me, God? GOD

is my life falling apa

Y DOES GOD LET BAD

Why, God? Why should I

d you let this happen?

od? WHY AM I SO ANXIOU

hy do bad things happen to go

WHY, GOD?

is there so much darkness?

wife get cancer?

NOTES

INTRODUCTION

1   President Franklin D. Roosevelt is widely credited with this quote based upon a portion of an inaugural address. However, with a slight modification, the quote is also attributed to Ambrose Hollingworth Redmoon in 1991. Nelson Mandela is also credited with a version of the quote.

TRUTH #1: GOD IS IN COMPLETE CONTROL

2   Abraham Kuyper; From his inaugural address entitled "Sphere of Sovereignty" at the dedication of Free University on October 20, 1880.

3   Phillips, J.B. Your God is Too Small. Chicago, Touchstone, June 1, 2004. Page 7.

4   Collins, Suzanne. The Hunger Games. New York, Scholastic, September 14, 2008.

5   Phillips, J.B. Your God is Too Small. Chicago, Touchstone, June 1, 2004. For more descriptions of false gods, read the first half of this book.

6   Allen, David. Christ-Centered Exposition: Exalting Jesus in Job. Holman Reference, Brentwood, April 15, 2022. Page 37.

7   Calvin, John. Institutes of the Christian Religion. Westminster Press, Louisville, June 1, 1960. Page 43.

8   Pink, A.W. The Sovereignty of God. Wilder Publications, Radford, March 26, 2009. Page 20.

9   Historian, United States Postal Service, (October 1999). Postal Service Mission and "Motto". USPS. https://about.usps.com/who/profile/history/pdf/mission-motto.pdf.

10   Barclay, William. The Daily Study Bible Series: The Gospel of Luke. Westminster Press, Louisville, January 1, 1977.

TRUTH #2: ALL THINGS EXIST FOR GOD'S GLORY

11   The Westminster Divines. The Westminster Shorter Catechism. Independently Published, January 30, 2023.

12   Chandler, Matt. [@TruthEndures] (2012, January 12). God is for God - Code Orange Revival. Youtube. https://youtu.be/9yqQuTT1S40?si=sQETT-eraheJowNM.

13   Saint Augustine. Confessions. Word on Fire Classics, Des Plaines, November 11, 2017. Page 5.

14   Piper, John; Edwards, Jonathan. God's Passion for His Glory: Living the Vision of Jonathan Edwards (With the Complete Text of The End for Which God Created the World). Crossway, Wheaton, January 6, 2006. Page 47.

15   Piper, John; Edwards, Jonathan. God's Passion for His Glory: Living the Vision of Jonathan Edwards (With the Complete Text of The End for Which God Created the World). Crossway, Wheaton, January 6, 2006. Page 33.

16   Piper, John; Edwards, Jonathan. God's Passion for His Glory: Living the Vision of Jonathan Edwards (With the Complete Text of The End for Which God Created the World). Crossway, Wheaton, January 6, 2006. Page 47.

TRUTH #3: GOD'S WAYS ARE NOT OUR WAYS

17   Cowper, William. William Cowper's Olney Hymns and Other Sacred Works. Curiosmith, Minneapolis, December 23, 2006. Page 63.

18   Lewis, C.S. Mere Christianity. HarperOne, San Francisco, February 6, 2001. Page 124.

19   Pink, A.W. The Sovereignty of God. Wilder Publications, Radford, March 26, 2009. Page 19.

20   Henley, William Ernest. A Selection of Poems. White Press, London, January 21, 2015, Page 96, Invictus.

21   Lord Acton. (19th Century). Acton Institute. https://www.acton.org/research/lord-acton-quote-archive

22   Edwards, Gene. A Tale of Three Kings: A Study in Brokenness. Tyndale House Publishers, Carol Stream, May 21, 1992.

23   Swindoll, Charles R. [@DallasTheologicalSeminary] (1992, May 21). God's School of Brokenness. Youtube. https://youtu.be/-0rZqnZ9cws?si=l-XUVi02m3s7Rkmo

24   Wilkerson, David. [@SermonIndex.net] (2012, August 5). A Call to Anguish. Youtube. https://youtu.be/NPPmpGFF5jE?si=qJj1rLYWfFkgadaX

25   Lewis, C.S. The Great Divorce. HarperOne, San Francisco, February 5, 2001. Page 69.

TRUTH #4: GOD LOVES YOU

26   Rhodes, Ron. 1001 Unforgettable Quotes about God, Faith, and the Bible. Harvest House Publishers, Eugene, April 1, 2011. Page 106.

27   Graham, Billy. The Quotable Billy Graham. Droke House, Anderson, January 1, 1966. Page 82.

28   Tozer, A.W. The Knowledge of the Holy - The Attributes of God: Their Meaning in the Christian Life. HarperOne, San Francisco, October 6, 2009. Page 105.

29   Nicholson,Martha Snell. (2016, March 18). WordPress/Bonhoefferblog. Guests. https://bonhoefferblog.wordpress.com/2016/03/18/guests-by-martha-snell-nicholson/.

30   Wood, Tony. (1995). Sometimes He Calms the Storm [Recorded by Scott Krippayne]. Wild Imagination, Word Records, Capitol CMG Publishing.

JESUS AND THE FOUR MOST IMPORTANT TRUTHS

31   Lawson, James Gilchrist. The Greatest Thoughts about Jesus Christ: Comp. from Many Sources. George H. Doran Company, Toronto, January 1, 1919. Page 81.

32   Tozer, A.W. The Knowledge of the Holy - The Attributes of God: Their Meaning in the Christian Life. HarperOne, San Francisco, October 6, 2009. Pages 117-118.

33   Greear, J.D. Stop Asking Jesus into Your Heart: How to Know for Sure You are Saved. B&H Publishing, Nashville, February 1, 2013. Page 16.

WHY? GOD!

34   Spurgeon, Charles. (2023, May 10). Prince of Preachers. https://www.princeofpreachers.org/quotable-quotes.html.

OUR VISION

Matthew 28:19-20: *"Go therefore and make disciples of all nations, baptizing them in the name of the Father and of the Son and of the Holy Spirit, teaching them to observe all that I have commanded you. And behold, I am with you always, to the end of the age."*

REACH

At The River Church, you will often hear the phrase, "We don't go to church, we are the Church." We believe that as God's people, our primary purpose and goal is to go out and make disciples of Jesus Christ. We encourage you to reach the world in your local communities.

GATHER

The goal of weekend gatherings at The River Church is to glorify Christ in all we do! Whether it be through singing, giving, serving, or any of the variety of ways He has gifted us and called us together, Jesus is at the center of it all. We celebrate that when followers of Christ gather together in unity, it's not only a refresher, it brings life-change!

GROW

Our Growth Communities are designed to mirror the early church in Acts as having *"all things in common."* They are smaller collections of believers who spend time together studying the Word, knowing and caring for one another relationally, and learning to increase their commitment to Christ by holding one another accountable.

The River Church
8393 E. Holly Rd.
Holly, MI 48442

theriverchurch.cc • info@theriverchurch.cc

Made in the USA
Monee, IL
28 September 2024

66165485R00081